Poems of C

Poems of
G. S. FRASER

Edited by Ian Fletcher and John Lucas

Leicester University Press

1981

First published in 1981 by Leicester University Press
Distributed in North America by Humanities Press Inc., New Jersey

Copyright © Leicester University Press 1981

Designed by Douglas Martin
Set in IBM Press Roman
Printed and bound in Great Britain by The Pitman Press, Bath

British Library Cataloguing in Publication Data
Fraser, G.S.
Poems of G.S. Fraser
I. Title II. Fletcher, Ian
III. Lucas, John
821'.912 PR1225

ISBN 0-7185-1214-6

Contents

The Traveller has Regrets (1948)

Translations

Introduction

George Sutherland Fraser was born on 8 November 1915 at Glasgow, where he attended school at the Glasgow Academy. A story of this period survives: on being awarded a prize, a child's version of *Don Quixote,* he opened it and began reading on his way down from the platform. In 1924 his father was appointed Deputy Town Clerk of Aberdeen, and George became a pupil at Aberdeen Grammar School. The following year the family took a pleasant eighteenth-century house just outside Aberdeen, with a rambling garden and large attic. George used the attic for telling elaborate stories and encouraging his younger sister to add her pocket money to his in order to buy books that were far too difficult for her to read. Nearby lived some cousins and George mounted plays and other entertainments of various levels of sophistication with his sister and cousins as cast.

In 1933 he was awarded a Bursary at St Andrews University, having received the Medal for Modern Languages at school, and in that same year he published his first article in a literary review. In his first year at St Andrews he won the annual competition for a one-act play about the death of Marlowe: *At the Mermaid.* Between 1936 and 1937 he edited the *St Andrews University Magazine,* publishing a socialist manifesto along with other contributions of which the authorities disapproved; the magazine was suppressed. Fraser left with 2nd Class Honours in Combined English and History in 1937. All his History papers fully merited a First, so one must assume that his views on English literature were heterodox.

Between 1937 and 1939, he worked as a trainee journalist on Aberdeen papers for a pound a week. Here he learnt sub-editing, all types of reporting, and was finally responsible for reviewing theatrical productions, films and writing leaders. This journalistic training certainly accounts for the speed and versatility of his prose. About his criticism there tends always to be something of the sense of an audience, an awareness of the topical in literary values.

In 1939, Fraser volunteered for military service on grounds of principle, but also, it seems, to please his father who the year before had been seriously ill. Called up for service just before Christmas 1939, Fraser was earmarked as a potential officer but was too awkward physically to be considered. Mustered into the Black Watch, he lived for a time in very squalid conditions in a disused dye works, working in the Company Office. In the late summer of 1940 he was transferred to the R.A.S.C. and sent outside London for training, but was actually in London during the night of the fire blitz of May 1941, slipping through without a pass to see his grandmother and aunt who lived in Neasden. The next week, he was embarked for Egypt.

In Cairo, between 1941 and 1942, Fraser worked on army publications and was promoted to sergeant and eventually to warrant officer. Another effort was made to steer him through O.C.T.U. but, although he performed admirably in written tests, he was still quite unable to assemble a rifle. He made many literary contacts in Cairo, most notably with the civilians associated with the magazine *Personal Landscape:* Lawrence Durrell, Bernard Spencer and Terence Tiller. He was also involved in the Salamander group clustered round Keith Bullen, nephew of A.H. Bullen, who was a schoolmaster in Cairo, a translator of Baudelaire and friend to poets, and generally managed to project on Cairo the image of a London literary Bohemia. Pubs were not frequent, but a little Greek grocer's shop, off Shama Solomon Pasha, became the local version of the Café Royal or the Wheatsheaf. It was here that Fraser met 'John Gawsworth' in transit to India, and many other service poets. Between 1943 and 1944 he served in Eritrea, editing the *Eritrea Daily News,* a half-Italian and half-English paper.

In 1943 he had published a pamphlet of poems with *Poetry London* and the following year, from the same publisher, appeared *Home Town Elegy.* In that same year he returned to Cairo as staff writer in the Ministry of Information, producing feature articles under the *nom de plume* of 'Atticus', that were widely reprinted in the local French, Arabic and Italian papers. He was now to be found in a musky crypt in the basement of the Ministry of Information building at Sharia Antikhana, and scandalized regimental sergeant majors by appearing in Kasr-El-Nil Barracks with his warrant officer's shield heavily tarnished and with wild bootlaces.

In December 1945 Fraser was demobilized and came back to Chelsea where his mother was living. The following year he married Eileen Lucy Andrew, by whom he had two daughters and a son. For the next thirteen years Fraser led an intensely active life as family man and as busy freelance journalist, contributing to such journals as *The New Statesman, Encounter, London Magazine,* writing numerous reviews and selecting poetry for the *Times Literary Supplement,* broadcasting for the B.B.C. Overseas Service and editing poetry programmes for the Third Programme. He also held an open evening for most weeks of the year at 75 Beaufort Street, Chelsea. Here, in the 1950s, generations of young poets came and read their works in an atmosphere that was sympathetic if somewhat chaotic. It was in this ambience that a number of those to be associated with the Movement and the Group were to be found. After each poem had been read, Fraser would sum up its virtues with a charitable lucidity. Something of his importance during that time may be gauged by Donald Davie's remark that for years G.S. Fraser was literary London's arbiter of poetic taste.

These strenuous years were broken by a long visit in 1947 to Uruguay, Argentina and Chile, where he stayed with Pablo Neruda. The fruit of these travels was a prose book, *News from South America,* and numerous accomplished translations from Neruda and other South American poets. From 1950 to 1951 Fraser was Cultural Adviser to the United Kingdom Liaison Mission in Japan, a task which made great demands on him. He was required to come to terms with a different culture and to turn his hand to teaching, lecturing and social contacts with Japanese of all kinds. Overwork brought on a total nervous breakdown, and it was some months before he could work again.

In January 1958 Fraser left London and the higher journalism on being appointed Lecturer in English at Leicester University; he was made Reader in Modern Literature in 1964, the title later being changed at his own request to Reader in Poetry. At Leicester, he was to be much involved with students' literary activities, poetry workshops and little magazines. His house in Guilford Road, Stoneygate, became as much a social centre as 75 Beaufort Street had been. He extended his role beyond the walls of the University and actively encouraged literary activities in the town.

In 1963-4, he was Visiting Professor at the University of Rochester, New York State, and besides contributing to the *New York Review of Books* and the *Partisan Review,* read his poems at Harvard, his chairman being I.A. Richards who, with Sir William Empson, had been perhaps the main formative influence on Fraser's criticism.

In 1974 Fraser suffered a heart attack, but recovered and was able to conduct his many activities until taking early retirement in the summer of 1979. He continued to advise his postgraduate students after retirement, remaining happy and busy until, after a short illness, he died on 3 January 1980.

2

In his substantial British Council pamphlet, *Poetry 1945-50,* published in 1951, Alan Ross discussed the poetry of G.S. Fraser in a chapter entitled 'Metaphysics and Redoubts'. Ross aligned Fraser with Ronald Bottrall, arguing that both poets typically thought in abstractions, and that they shared a certain number of intellectual preoccupations. However, Ross considered Fraser to be the 'smoother and clearer' poet, and he also claimed that

> Fraser's best poems, those nearest to life and with solid roots in experience, are those with early origins in his native Scotland: where his poetic feeling comes from observation and memory, not from acquaintance with literature.

It is of course true that from first to last Fraser had a liking for the poetry of abstract terms. No doubt his Scottish education had much to do with his enjoyment of and skill at puzzles, riddles and logic games; and as Sir William Empson has pointed out, Fraser was a most accomplished 'argufier' in verse. As examples of this one could cite the early 'Utopia and Ideology', 'Yin and Yang', or the brilliant 'The Insane Philosophers', which, while it owes something to Wallace Stevens, is nevertheless a poem such as only Fraser could write.

Yet Ross's account of Fraser hardly does justice to him, and not merely because Fraser's attitude to Scotland was a good deal more complex than Ross implies. 'To Hugh MacDiarmid' ends with Fraser rejecting one kind of 'native Scotland'.

> Because my love was never for the common
> But only for the rare, the singular air,
> Or the undifferenced and naked human,
> Your Keltic mythos shudders me with fear.

> What a race has is always crude and common,
> And not the human or the personal:
> I would take sword up only for the human,
> Not to revive the broken ghosts of Gael.

A bit priggish, to be sure. But clearly enough Fraser feared that to see Scotland in terms of certain political or literary causes could lead only to a constricting of the free life of the imagination; and that there was more substance in the enmity than in the love of Scottish nationalist poetics. Equally clearly, Fraser's powers of observation and memory are not exhausted by the country which he left in early manhood, and to which he never returned for any length of time.

As for 'clearer and smoother': such faint praise comes a long way short of accounting for Fraser's great metrical variousness, his deep knowledge and use of a wide range of verse forms, and above all that subtle sense of rhythm of which he was so justly proud. Besides, it is surely the case that many of Fraser's finest poems – and they are very fine indeed – come precisely from his 'acquaintance with literature'? This is not to say that he was a literary poet in the bad sense. Rather, his extensive reading in the poetry of many languages and cultures gave him the opportunity to develop his art by reference to, and absorption of, a number of models.

Yeats was pre-eminent among these, sometimes too much so. In a late, beautiful poem, 'Colleagues and Students', Fraser speaks of being

> the trumpet through which
> A great dead man can sound
> With a hound-in-cry's voice: ...

And like the Shelley whom he recalls in that image of the trumpet, his readiness to hero-worship, in his case Yeats, occasionally drowned the sound of his own voice. More, in the early verse there are obtrusive borrowings from Auden. But then what poet beginning to write in the late 1930s could hope to escape *that* influence?

Yet these unassimilated echoes and borrowings do not intrude into the bulk of his work. At his best, Fraser's voice is an utterly distinctive one. It is the voice of a man at once wrily witty, capable of anger, but modest, knowledgeable though, curious, vulnerable; most valuably, perhaps, it is a voice that is marked by a kind of off-hand conversational eloquence, an eager desire to communicate. In short it is the true Horatian voice, and although Fraser came to write about one of its great English exemplars, Pope, only at the end of his life, and expressed some misgivings about Auden, who is another, there seems no doubt that the Horatian mode appealed to him from the outset, and that he was always able to command it. That is why he wrote so many 'letter' poems, beginning with the 'Letter to Anne Ridler' and the charming 'Christmas Letter Home' in *Home Town Elegy,* and continuing right the way through to the work of the last decade. Many other poems are best thought of as conversation poems; they presume an interested reader, one willing to argue back. For much that is most attractive about such poems – their lucidity, their vulnerable generosity of statement – depends on the poet's sense that what he says is contingent, open-ended. It is after all difficult to read poems like 'Home Thoughts on Ireland' or 'A Performance of *The Bacchae*' without wanting to dispute some points. Which is as the poems intend.

At its truest such poetry is intensely civilized. Fraser's best poems, whether they are love poems, elegies, epistolary or philosophic, have a sweetness of regard for subject and auditor that is the hallmark of a most civilized man. This is not the same as sentimentality. For although Fraser sometimes comes near to the merely soft, a certain astringent wit usually steers him away from sogginess. For example, the 'Elegy for Keith Bullen':

> Keith was particularly Sunday morning,
> Red roses, old brandy, was unharrying Time,
> Was that white light, our youth; or was the fawning
> Zephyr that bobs the gay balloon of Rhyme,
>
> He bobbed incredibly in our modern air;...

These lines very finely evoke a particular presence. It is partly a matter of the substituted word, unharrying for unhurrying, which pays tribute to a social virtue while recognizing its olde-worldliness, partly a matter of the satiric hint that is contained in the word 'incredibly' (he was incredible to us, we were incredible to him); and partly the sly fastidiousness of 'particularly'. Between them, such words gently mock and honour the man. And in that marvellous poem 'For Tilly, Sick, With Love', Fraser's dexterity in handling a difficult metre allows his voice a range of tones that means it need never settle for the merely sentimental/solemn. The graceful anapests repeatedly lift it clear of the more predictable, weighty, iambic measure. Presumably the poem owes something to Browning's great 'A Toccata of Gallupi's', but Fraser's virtuosity is his own. 'For Tilly, Sick, With Love' is a poem of consummate craft.

Fraser wrote much poetry during the 1940s and most of the 1950s, but the 1960s seems to have been a comparatively barren decade. There are doubtless a number of reasons for this. He put a great deal of work into his University commitments; he may have felt that his move to Leicester coincided with the arrival of younger poets on the literary scene, and that he was no longer sure of an audience. And after all poets do go through dull or arid patches, especially in middle age. At all events, the 1970s saw a remarkable late flowering, and much of his best work was written during that decade.

3

When we began to prepare this edition we hoped to provide more or less accurate dating for each poem. In the event this proved impossible. We have, however, tried to make sure that the poems appear in chronological order. And we have added notes whenever they seemed essential. But the present volume is obviously not intended as a definitive edition. For one thing, many of the previously unpublished or uncollected poems exist in a number of different drafts, and it was not always clear which was the final one, or the one the poet preferred. For another, some published or collected poems were subsequently altered (and here we have usually preferred the earlier version). Thirdly, there may well be poems in obscure journals which we have failed to track down. And finally, the present volume omits a large number of very fine translations from, among other languages, the French and Italian. It is to be hoped that a volume of Fraser's translations will be undertaken some time in the future.

The editors wish to acknowledge the help they have received from Paddy Fraser, without whom this volume could not have been accomplished.

Ian Fletcher
John Lucas

Poems from
The Fatal Landscape
1943

The Fatal Landscape was published by Poetry London (P.L. Pamphlet No. 3) in 1943. All the poems in this pamphlet were later included in *Home Town Elegy,* published by Poetry London in 1944, with the exception of the three which follow: 'Social Pleasures', 'Problems of a Poet' and 'Early Spring'.

Social Pleasures

The Orchestra starts, slowly, I crush my stub,
I rise and I wait till the others
Have chosen their partners, and awkwardly
I smile, I say, 'May I?' she smiles faintly,
We move off stiffly, and...

Bunny perhaps, with her smooth dark hair, her pale
Heavily powdered skin, her little
Rabbit's smile, and the agreeable pressure
Of a fully-developed body. 'Well, George,
Been working hard lately?' 'Oh the usual,
The hours are long but the work is light.'
And, 'Really, you are dancing better lately.'
And a stiff bow at the end, 'Thank you, thank you.'

Bunny, the Giaconda of her province,
Inspiring durable and awkward affections:
With her little refined drawl, her pale smile,
Mystery behind a little malicious chatter
And maybe nothing at all behind mystery.
But then I have never seen her playing her game:
Heavy, and awkward, and dull, for her I am
Part of the burden, an old friend of the family.

Or perhaps Joy, with the charm
Of a creamy parchment skin on a neat skull;
The dark large pupils of unfocussed eyes,
And the honey voice, sticky in its sweetness.
Breaking with Joy, after the dance, I run
My hand down her pale warm arm;
Dancing, I am always thoroughly aware
Of the delicate contact of her small fingers.
I compliment her on her dress, ask her
About dances, parties, pictures. She sighs,
She didn't do so well in exams this term.

Or perhaps, Sheila, the thorough sportsman,
With her strong jaw and her boy's smile,
Abrupt, humorous. The music stops,
Then starts again. Falling in with her style,
'Anyway, I rather like holding you like this.'
She jeers back, 'How kind of you to say so!'

Or Rosemary, with her sunburn powder,
Her dark lipstick, her daintiness,
And her literary gossip. At Malvern
She bumped deliberately into Hugh Walpole,
Just to make him start and say 'Excuse me!'
She saw Bernard Shaw outside the theatre,
All alone, poring with simple vanity
Over his latest batch of photographs.
Or Italy, and the charm of Count Ciano,
Or Grenoble, and a mad Hungarian,
Who used to say for a joke that in Hungary
They ate young girls for breakfast, tea and dinner.
He was a cousin of the Archduke Otto,
And that was the week of the Soviet-German pact.
He absolutely hated Ribbentrop...

Those are the lucky who, like Fritz and Freddy,
Know what to say to girls, and know
Just what to feel about them. I hardly know
What exactly to say or what to feel.
The orchestra starts slowly, I crush my stub,
I rise, and I wait till the others
Have chosen their partners, and awkwardly
I smile, I say, 'May I?' She smiles faintly,
We move off stiffly.

I worry much about my quarter-turns.
I ask, 'Is this a waltz or a slow fox-trot?'
I see them looking down occasionally
To see what I am doing with my feet.
And, 'You can walk all over me,' says Sheila,
'I am as tough as a rhinoceros.'
'Shall we sit this one out?' says Bunny.

And later, trying to write lyric poems,
Expressing some intense and simple passion,
I muse upon these fragmentary contacts;
And remember a sentence of Louis MacNeice,
In *The Arts Today,* that in poetry
'One cannot force the empirical element.'
I remember a green net dress of Rosemary's
But find it makes a poor show in a poem.

Then, not for the first time certainly, I wish,
I glumly wish, at birth I had been given
A rasher, more impetuous temperament
And a less cautious, hesitating mind.

I meditate on Nicky and Lord Byron.
Stare at the typewriter and crush my stub.
The metre starts in my head, I type stiffly.

And it doesn't turn into a dance or a poem.

Problems of a Poet

Strange that so young I should carry only
A civil mask and a handful of talents.
Strange that the 'I' should have done so soon.

No wonder the mask and the handful are lonely.
No wonder I wander, a crazy loon,
By the shining pavements and the duller moon,
Seeking a poem for my handful of talents.

'What will you write about? Trees, politics, women...'
I shall write about nothing at all.
They shall say, his basket was emptied early,
He bowed, but did not come for the curtain call.

With my assured income and my smart pen,
Smug and successful, but all the more desperately
Seeking a poem for my handful of talents,
I shall wander among the cushions, the stuffed men...

'Yes,' I shall say, 'the late Sir Osbert Sitwell,
I knew that famous wit well.
I knew him in his dark and gouty years...
Yes, all his verses make as fat a book as
Those of his enemy, old Frankie Lucas.
But lady, are these deaths a thing for tears?'

19

I shall make conversation
I shall make conversation
Out of the twigs that twitter in the breeze,
Out of fantastic fables such as these.
I shall make conversation
Out of the varied surface of inane vexation
With the women who have sweet and cooing voices,
Who have soft plump hands. I shall wander
Into the ballroom, under the candelabra,
And admire the paper rhododendrons, and admire
The hair of the head upon the shoulder.

The poem is there, the poem is not in the distance,
For in this too heroic age, alas,
I never swam the Channel, crossed the Ebro,
Or fasted for a year on meadow grass:
Old men admire me for a pleasant manner,
Old men admire me for a 'balanced' air...
I gawk at the mechanic with his spanner
I goggle at the air-plane in the air,
I listen to the harsh and simple voices
Of all the advertisers selling death...
I turn to the Sheilas and the Joyces,
The sweet inaneness of their cooing breath.

Early Spring

Now the field of the sea
Where the foam was white daisies,
Lurks like the lava-floe,
Lies like treacle and lazes,
And the moaning sea-birds go
Towards the winter's wake.
Cruel life begins to flow,
Murderous ash-buds break.

Nearer the skin, the blood
Is tender at day's dawning,
Feeling the chintz on the glass
Of the green banks yawning,
Sharp as the green grass,
And taking the old hurt.
The film is scrapped, the dreams pass,
The question is curt.

And drinking the white light
I meditate an answer,
Whether it means death,
Slow death, like cancer,
Or whether it means new breath,
New courage to fail.
The green beaks of the buds have faith,
To them it is a new tale.

Home Town Elegy
1944

The Fatal Landscape

That is the face of a man going into action. It is a little different from any other face that you will ever see.
Hemingway, in 'Spanish Earth'.

Death, though darkly present
In these declining vales,
Smiles and looks pleasant
As the photo fails

And the spying eye
Carries away
A trophy, too faint to dye
The wholesome air of day:

But melting on the night
The cloudy negative,
With our own lust alight,
Half consents to give.

As sleep comes on,
The unhesitating hand
Plucking the sun of dawn
And the sky to understand.

But the enormous landscape
Darkens, and blind
With terror of its own rape,
The scene outstares the mind:

Till the wished-for valley is
Inverted tripod, curl of mist
Outlining bones as hard as this
Steel that the bones resist.

Tribute

Darling, I see the innocent murderers
Bursting upon Time's tree, a smile like hers
Who breaks the greener casing of the air
With love, and leaves a sticky menace there.
I have broken these little buds from the spring tree,
And there still are leaves, and nothing has happened to me,
I have torn the blooms from the branch in later spring,
And the fruit still flourishes, the birds still sing,
I have shaken down from the bough the ripened fruit
And winter has not withered the tree's root.

In summer I have lain by the water
And watched the sleek devices of the otter
And killed the cubs, their blood has bathed the pool,
And yet I live and find the breezes cool,
Darling, Time is iniquity's enemy
And the healing touch of time is kind to me.

God in heaven, I hear, in the old days
Was set to proclaim the punishment of our ways
And his son was sent among us to gather our guilt,
And on that one tree, the blood of the world was spilt,
And now there is no God, and who can forgive us, unless
We accord to each other mutual forgiveness?

And you who could forgive me what I seem
Are too noble for constrained fears and the dream,
You exist in time, you exist apart from me,
And your Time will never be my Eternity.

Poem for a Play

Summer, you say, is fallen like a feather,
The stippled birches stripped, and black the heather.
The mind is moaning for that better weather
   As you moan.
Say summer is your mind, the tree your lover,
Then winter is the damnèd doubts that hover:
Death, when the hawk swoops and the doubts are over,
   A dropped stone.

Let not the stone drop. Let the hawk
High in the sky whom your eyes mock
(As glances of courtesans mock, mock)
Let him fly in fear
To another quarry, away from the hawk
Of your mockery. Mock, mock
Till death is afraid to drop a stone on a stone.

Two Short Poems

I

Shadows darken the soft line
Of the valley, blot trees and streams
Running like ice among the snows
That freeze with fear the lover's dreams.
Far off, on his rock the rains whine,
Here the top of his desolate tower shows.

Shadows break, and day is bright
In the grey and melting valley,
Steamy in the morning sun, soon dry
Of snows, and with one deep gully
Drinking the little streams as dark as night.
The tower is hidden in the misty morning sky.

II

Summer is gone with strawberries.
Haremburgis, that held the Maine,
Is gone and will not come again.
Youth is fair but beauty flies,
Dust hath closèd Helen's eyes.
Words we scrawl that Time, like rain,
Washes from the window-pane.
Nobody will express surprise.

Ah, my sister, let's not dream,
Like a boy who butts the wind,
Time will ne'er be less unkind.
Gaze not in the crystal stream,
Lilies none, nor leaves, it yields.
Winter savages the fields.

Elegy

(From Albert Samain)

When night upon the sky her sadness pours,
And you, so pale upon the balcony,
Detach that sign from time and its decay,
Your placid face, my simple heart adores.

Now, at the hour when all the lamps are lit,
The town, where noises one by one decay,
Deserted falls back faint and far away,
And old medallions have the look of it.

Sad, we are silent. Sometimes one word lingers,
A brittle bridge, where soul to soul may speak.
The sky is stained, the charm is unique...
This flight of time, it seems, between our fingers.

And here I could remain for hours, for nights,
For years I think, and have my only care
To nurse that head, that heavy weight of hair,
That now seems dead among the faded lights.

It is the lake where twilight sleeps for ever,
The well-side seat, the nap among rich flowers;
Such golden threads bind thoughts to things, and ours
Under the shuttle shake with a long shiver.

O keep this hour among all hours and days...
So that its memory, like powdered scent,
When we are weary of the ways we went
At nights may comfort us on wearier ways.

The gardens of the night are all in flower.
Lines, colours, little noises die away.
Your rings are tortured with the light's last ray...
Sister, it is some creature's passing-hour!

Against my brow your hands, pure water, melt;
Over my eyes your hands, fresh flowers, are sweet.
My soul, where all the springs of sorrow meet,
A pallid faithful lily in your belt.

Though all the earth is mounting with our sighs,
'Tis Pity that puts thus her hand on us.
So sad and sweet, to me delirious,
You say this with your heaven-erected eyes.

Elegy for Certain Resolutions

My arrowy flights, more speed than solace,
Depart: they feel, I know, like swallows,
Summer decay and this cold trunk survive,
And in this leafless intricate tracery
Only tough bark and crystalline frost will thrive.
I now no more can dream
To drink new life of the habitual stream
Or in the hail that beats upon my head:
It is not just the summer's finery,
The leaf and flower, token of a green tree,
It is the sap and energy are dead.

I used to ride upon a horse, with reins
Curved in the fingers of a feeble hand,
Would play at single-stick on Saturdays,
Had Algebra and Euclid to understand:
Shirker of Rugby, swam — refrains,
Timed to the half-learned swimmer's arm that plies
To carve the water into precious stones,
Of Keats and Shelley, many a phrase,
Bursting like mercury before my eyes...
And every season toughening my bones.

Lay ill! how long, and heard strange trains,
Perhaps the seething of my brains,
Rumbling on winter afternoons,
At four o'clock had tea with scones,
And while I ate lapped up detective stories:
Aware obscurely of the purple quilt,
The small square tea-tray with the sugar spilt,
But more directly of the admiring chorus
Of Parker to Lord Peter Wimsey's tricks,
And the unburied body pacing Styx...

An enormous vista opened out before me.
This acquaintance to make, this truth to asseverate,
Nothing could be too difficult or bore me:
I should find out all about ethics, logic, science...
Only at night the small print sneered defiance!
Then as the studious eye grew duller,
And as the heavy head grew fuller,
Life quickened less under the sensitive hand...
The ear began to fumble for the beat,
The mind was lost in the syntax of Latin prose:
The memory overburdened with words and words
Came to the stage where the single vision curds
And a frozen peep-show photo is all one knows.

'To live by feeling!' One had to countermand
That order, finding the tact for the matter gone.
No longer so strangely the sun shone
In the dark northern winter. Quiet the brood
Of sorrows, now — beneath too calm a hood!

Poem

Ask me no more where the rose is.
Summer constrains,
As winter sleeks and gloses
With opaque pains
The mud and the little fishes,
And the rock is not revived by the old rains,
The grey roots grip where there are no wishes.

For now winter is falling,
Soft and warm, like silks from a woman, the snow.
By the warm house, the well-loved voice is calling,
But home I shall not go.

Tactics

Sometimes the look of a head, a sort
Of poise of interest without insolence —
Sometimes out of a wise consort
A fool talks sense!
Sometimes enmity brings no grief,
After argument, teeth are shown,
We bear no malice, we bridge belief,
Our thoughts are our own.
Not always alone we bear the yoke,
Sometimes the little private joke,
Is public wit, the crabbed word
A flag code for the naval eye,
The confided nightmare not absurd.
Defying only with a smile
Assures you here's no enemy
Though we meet in a narrow mile
And one must pass and one must die,
Defying only, until a sigh
Or a soft gesture or a word
Assures the doomed, *No enemy:*
All defences are absurd.

Utopia and Ideology [1]

Become a pastoral privacy,
      You with your curving paths and lawns,
For happy wanderers: not for me
      To sip the stream and pet the bridling swans.

Darling, you know this story, you know time
      Under the sycamore, the willow whorls —
That love-song, 'Will the year repeat its prime?'
      But winter hangs all white upon the laurels.

Beauty, and every bronze eternal tree.
      Your smile and word, your turning to escape,
Speak of a hidden valley, what to me
      Is only spoil of Dis's gloomy rape.

Some way to set the world to rights with arms
      Withers the natural centres at the core,
As in a myth I see your paper charms
      And sigh, and turn the page, and sigh no more.

Love died in Troy when Helen was the rage;
      The natural care for kindness. They who are
On this partitioned and revolving stage
      Movers, fight not for Helen in this war.

Birthday Greeting

(April 20th, 1939)

Recurrent and recurrent in that corridor
Fifty tall chimneys weeping their vain tears,
Staining the fingers that defend each tower
From headlong falling and from father's shears

Whose threats, like scissoring searchlights, cut
The soaring airman's scarlet challenge down,
The caballero horned by the brute
And sprawled in ruins on the smoking town,

Whose smoke-clouds screen nerves' panic-stricken runners;
You also are their hands, that bless the wrath
Of the steel cylinder, whose amorous honours
Are counted not in birth but multiple death.

You the defender and attacker are
The common symbol of love quarantined
Within one body, weary of that war
Where all retreats and feints are predivined:

Yours is the power of the too long unloved,
Of the contorted eye-ball, and the sick
Throat, whose vibrant loneliness has moved
Sleek loins and bowels to shudder for your lack

Of all that strokes and soothes and leaves at peace
The labyrinth of sorrows and the flower
That shrinks from daylight, but finds no release
Denied the dark sun of its darker hour.

Hitler, your war potential is the image
Of the blind windows and the smoky years
In lost Vienna, for whose permanent damage
Dreams wet your spartan pillow with weak tears.

Lust, that the poet figures as a lily,
A towering lily, a receptive rose,
Hardens for you to one tall factory-chimney
Whose war-mad furnace roars without repose...

And now you are a universal father,
Strange focus of the polar love and hate
Of these stiff, nervous children whom you gather
To shear the shiny fifty-candled cake.

Two Sonnets

Leaving her I loved in the picturesque winter
Flanked by cathedrals and daunted by the north sea
To celebrate alone the vernal festival,
I returned, I wept. In the mind I could not stint her
Of the swans or cypresses, I found that all
My memories of her face and words were woven
Into a pattern of an intricate delicacy,
A tapestry, where a formal wind had driven
Many an unapproached, an agonising head;
There that girl's gold soon-stained medallion, there
The cold symmetrical features of the bluecoat boy,
There all desires forgotten and dreams half-dead...
But that one face that might have made me joy,
Where had her paleness gone, and her black stare?

For like the monuments which commemorate
By a suave lion in an inscribed alcove
Pain and the loneliness of sodden fields
Where war's protracted deaths have punctured hate
To whimper like a baby as it yields,
My poems were a lie about my sorrow;
The complicated miseries of love
Were smoothed by them. These other miseries borrow
Similarly false glory for the slain
From mock-heroics that console a nation.
Pain is too cheap a gift to give to pain.
The intricacy of the exposed intestines
Presents no easy formal inspiration
Till art disguises them as wreathing vines.

Lean Street

Here, where the baby paddles in the gutter,
    Here in the slaty greyness and the gas,
Here where the women wear dark shawls and mutter
    A hasty word as other women pass,

Telling the secret, telling, clucking and tutting,
    Sighing, or saying that it served her right,
The bitch! — the words and weather both are cutting
    In Causewayend, on this November night.

At pavement's end and in the slaty weather
    I stare with glazing eyes at meagre stone,
Rain and the gas are sputtering together
    A dreary tune! O leave my heart alone,

O leave my heart alone, I tell my sorrows,
    For I will soothe you in a softer bed
And I will numb your grief with fat to-morrows
    Who break your milk teeth on this stony bread!

They do not hear. Thought stings me like an adder,
    A doorway's sagging plumb-line squints at me,
The fat sky gurgles like a swollen bladder
    With the foul rain that rains on poverty.

Elegy

Many I pursued and from a distance
Many admired. Her whose curls were cold serpents,
Whose profile was a steel medallion,
But whose complexion one term tired.

Whose voice from her throat was ghostly
As wood-blue smoke, as the smoke from a bonfire,
But who sadly decayed from beauty
Into mere distinction. A fire of coke.

Also I loved a shallow bluecoat boy
Who for a man was much too beautiful,
Whose triviality then tinkled with a
Bell-like brightness, and could almost fan

A mind made curious by such symmetry,
Whose warm life then played on him like sunlight
On an apple, made his shallow flippancies
As wounding as wit's lean knife.

Poem

(after André Breton)

Under the parasol the prostitute is pretty,
Her rather shabby summer dress the echoing colour of the woods:
She carries with her a big fragment of wall-paper,
A torn scrap, such as we see with sorrow
On the third floor of an old condemned house:
They have broken down the wall to let us see it.
Or she may carry a twiddle of white marble
Fallen from the mantle, or a stucco wreath, or
Gilded chains, such as burn in mirrors,
For fire walks on the hot pavements where she walks,
Like a flower that has been fried.
Her eyes hold off a far-off wind of stone,
Her eyes see the centre of the wind-storm,
Too stony, still, and deep.

Nothing can touch me more
Than these thoughts in those eyes,
These stamps unlicked:
A fresh stream flows of shadow, where her heels
Trample the dead shadow of her head.
I think of her, fingered and dropped
By all the hands that finger
As you clutch and you drop fistfuls of chopped hay.
The night is dark, is deep. Only her breasts
Rise like the sun, and that falling and rising
Measures her night and day:
They are like stars upon the huge blue waters
And ever unappeased their blue milk keens.

A Night

(after Giorgio de Chirico)

Last night the wind blew so hard I believed it was
      going to crush the rocks like a paste-board packet.
All the time the electric lights of the darkness
Burned like hearts.
In the third sleep I awoke near the lake
Where came to die the water of two rivers.
Round the table women were reading.
And the monk was quiet in the shade.
Slowly I passed the bridge and below mirk water
I saw passing slowly great black fish.
All at once I found myself in a great square town.
All the windows were closed, everywhere was silence,
Everywhere meditation.
And the monk again passed beside me. Through the holes
      of his rotten robe I saw the beauty of his body
      pale and white like a statue of love.
On waking happiness once again slept beside me.

.

Image in Lamplight

I crane my neck and I look up.
A branch is craning down to me
Whose frail and floating bubbles sup
Upon that dark electric sea.

The buds are bubbles of green glass
Under the blue lamp's flattering glow.
The empty sky above might pass
For satin stained with indigo.

It is the bulb's electric blue
And not the branch and not the sky.
It is your costume and not you.
It never is the obvious why.

I muse on the irrelevant
And on the subtle tricks of chance
That make a poet lean and gaunt
And frame his mind to elegance.

Tramp's Song

'Some window makes a smear, a blur of yellow light
On walls that disappear under the wash of night,'
The lean dogs are howling to the moon.

'Under my worn heel the wet bright pavements skid.
Loud hail-drops peal on the ash-can's tin lid,'
The lean dogs are howling to the moon.

'I might have had fat stew and slept in a soft bed
If the small good I knew had not moidered my head,'
The lean dogs are howling to the moon.

'O, who will patch up Time, that worn old dish-rag?
Who will give me a dime? Who will spare me a fag?'
The lean dogs are howling to the moon.

'I looked at solid men, I saw their wits were crazed,
And when I left them then, my heart with honour blazed,'
The lean dogs are howling to the moon.

'Time had a better season. I clasped my doxies close
And called my follies reason so high my follies rose,'
The lean dogs are howling to the moon.

'Time had a better season. Time is an old dish-rag.
You who prosper by treason, spare a poet a fag'
The lean dogs are howling to the moon.

For Yeats

I am that seed whose sorrow's song is sorrow,
I am that blood whose beauty's death is bane,
I am the mourner of the orator
And the lamenter of the actor's plume;
My words must have a ribboned elegance
Like the blue chiffon of the swirling smoke
Whose pattern is the eddy of the weather
Within the sunny, curtained drawing-room.
The age piles up its ash, our words
Are smoke that swirls in acridness.
Yours was the head that could forgive this folly;
Your sure hand from the heart's decaying meat
Built the glazed eye's undying monument.
And mine, alas, the dry, dissecting mind
Inhabited by monsters, like this insect
With small wings and elegant body
And two incomprehensible antennae
Starting out of its tail, crawling
On the inhibiting and translucent pane.
I dramatise the world you never noticed.
Mine was the eye to which the noble
Symbols, the adoration
Of a woman for the first time, which is like
An ache against the shoulders,
Or like the drowning hopelessness of dreams,
Or the mad symbols, the manse's
Stunted trees in Peterhead, and the hollow
Chimney-pots laid on one side for a wall,
To make a noise like the wind soughing in trees,
Promised revelation and revealed impotence,
Promised wisdom and revealed perplexity.
Dry trees, and rocks, streams, eagles, and riders
Crying for vengeance on the murderers
Of Jacques de Molay, these were your voice.
You were at home with mad and noble symbols;
You gave me muscles I had never used,
As if your verses taught me how to swim.
And much I mourn in my sorrow's morning
That out of vegetative grief,
Out of growing like a tree, stunted
By its own dream in the water,
I tore no image fit to meet your eye.
Thinking of you, I turn from this day
And from our thwarted tongues, our minds
That grapple with the expedient and humane,
Towards the sorrows of Byzantium
And these metallic names on Gibbon's page:

Once more blind Belisarius, and once more
Old savage Narses, crying out in pain,
'I will now spin Her Resplendancy such a thread
As she will not unravel soon again!'
I think of these half-barbarous heroes, who
In Tunis, Persi and the Lombard plain
Held utter barbarism back, and then
Were spurned by the corrupted; Belisarius,
His eyes pricked out with needles, saying
'Spare a copper for the conqueror.
Spare a penny for Belisarius,
Who saved you from the Vandals and the Lombards,
Who saved you from the swarms of the East!'
And Narses, angry with a woman's sneer,
Lays down his arms, bids the tide flow in:
Like these anachronistic figures, you
Seemed a man greater than your loyalties,
But your mind saw it; and you made
A pattern of the history of our time,
And praised us for such virtues as we had:
Your perfect pity gilded your disdain.
'Things fall apart, the centre cannot hold...'
And you who made your strange centrality
Of outworn myths and outworn politics
And a sophistical philosophy
Leave no successor who might wear that cloak.

I salute you, in departing, as I salute
Don Juan, when he takes
The marble hand of the Commander's statue...
It is long since I rode on horseback,
Since I struck back at an insult
With an unforgiving will;
It is long since my heart felt sick,
And fierce joy in the sickness,
Because of some beauty's casual,
Casual and kind words. Now, I accept it,
I am a man of my age, poet!
Nerves, exasperation, and pity!
Graphs and blueprints, and the glib
Verbalism, my guts swallow
The indigestible abstractions,
'The terrible stone dolls.'
Plausible, verbose, humane,—
You were the last of my 'certain' men
And I shall never feel sure again.

To My Friends

(on leaving St Andrews, summer of 1937)

We, born too late, in this unlucky age,
When charm and honesty had left the stage,
    Must watch heroic honour rant alone;
And yet we have controlled our politic rage
    And argued, sometimes, in an easy tone...
This little town from out the turbid tide
That lashes Britain, beating far and wide
    The ancient rocks with a still-threatening wave,
    We, whom the brass of war had not made brave,
By mask, by trick of manner or of wit,
    We saved! Or do they need to learn to save
Who safe, and ignorant, and sheltered sit?

So soon our trifling treaties have an end
These thoughts seem oak, though willow-like they bend...
    The real world waits us. 'Tis a rougher place,
Marshalled for marching. Here, they choose a friend
    Not for the careless talent, casual grace,
But bearing still in mind the crucial day
When pain and noise must batter out a way
    Here, in dead earnest, in no fit or start —
    O, batter where here? Here, we'll take our part
Not with the scribbler's paper, orator's breath,
    But solid arguments to touch the heart,
New logic; I mean, anger, hate, and death.

Such is our doom, we scholars. Honour comes
Always with marching feet and noise of drums,
    Music to drown the voice of common reason!
When life with hate, when time with anger hums
    Perhaps to think too coolly is a treason
To some new Caesar... Brutus was his friend
But thought too coolly and so made an end
    Of that great man of the democracy.
    Purse-proud patrician, empty reasoner he!
Traitor to justice and the common man!
    Cool reason paid the price at Philippi.
O scholars, back the winner while you can!

Meditation of a Patriot

The posters show my country blonde and green,
Like some sweet siren, but the travellers know
How dull the shale sky is, the airs how keen,
And how our boorish manners freeze like snow.
Romantic Scotland was an emigrant,
Half-blooded, and escaped from sullen weather.
Here, we toss off a dram to drown a cough
And whisky has the trade-mark of the heather.
My heart yearns southwards as the shadows slant,
I wish I were an exile and I rave:
    With Byron and with Lermontov
    Romantic Scotland's in the grave.

In Glasgow, that damned sprawling evil town,
I interview a vulgar editor,
Who, brawny, self-made, looks me up and down
And seems to wonder what my sort is for.
Do I write verse? Ah, man, but that is bad...
And, too polite, I fawn upon this tough,
But when I leave him, O my heart is sad.
He sings alone who in this province sings.
I kick a lamp-post, and in drink I rave:
    With Byron and with Lermontov
    Romantic Scotland's in the grave.

In the far islands to the north and west
Mackenzie and MacDiarmid have their peace.
St Andrews soothes that critic at her breast
Whose polished verse ne'er gave his soul release.
I have no islands and no ancient stone,
Only the sugary granite glittering crisp
Pleases the eye, but turns affection off,
Hard rhetoric, that never learned to lisp.
This town has beauty, but I walk alone
And to the flat and sallow sands I rave:
    With Byron and with Lermontov
    Romantic Scotland's in the grave.

To Hugh MacDiarmid

Since mine was never the heroic gesture,
    Trained to slick city from my childhood's days,
Only a rambling garden's artful leisure
    Giving my mind its privacy and ease,

Since Poverty for me has never sharpened
        Her single tooth, and since Adversity
So far has failed to jab me with her hair-pin
        I marvel who my Scottish Muse can be.

I am Convention's child, the cub reporter,
        The sleek, the smooth, conservatively poised:
Abandoned long ago by Beauty's daughter;
        Tamed like a broncho, and commercialised!

Perhaps I have a heart that feels... I wonder!
        At least I can salute your courage high,
Your thought that burns language to a cinder,
        Your anger, and your angry poet's joy.

O warrior, with the world and wind against you,
        Old sea-bird, in your bleak and rocky coign,
Only my fears can follow where you fly to...
        Beneath these rocks, how many souls lie slain!

Your journey has not been the private journey
        Through a mad loveliness, of Hölderlin.
Against the windmills, sir, you choose to tourney.
        And yet, by marvellous chance, you hold your own.

O true bright sword! Perhaps, like Mithridates,
        Before the night has fallen, you may say:
Now I am satisfied: at least, my hate is:
        Now let me die: I saw the English flee.

Facing boys' faces, whom your world of thunder
        Is massing clouds for, whom the violet forks
Seek out from heaven...simulating candour
        I face both ways! A secret question carks.

Because my love was never for the common
        But only for the rare, the singular air,
Or the undifferenced and naked human,
        Your Keltic mythos shudders me with fear.

What a race has is always crude and common,
        And not the human or the personal:
I would take sword up only for the human,
        Not to revive the broken ghosts of Gael.

Poem

Now cry your heart out if you can,
Cry for many a simple man.
I would weep, too, for my part,
But too soon I drained my heart,
Seeing only beauty could
Rouse or touch my tender blood,
Seeing that my coward will
Kept me far from beauty still
And my awkward limbs and tongue
Were not framed to charm the young;
Seeing all that beauty had
Time and circumstance forbade
Me to touch or me to taste,
Seeing all my youth ran waste.
Many a fool as dull as I
Now must rouse himself to die,
Now must seek a colder bed
Than the loneliest he had
Now must learn to lie alone
In the nakedness of bone,
Or through nights of terror wake
When harder things than hearts can break;
When the inventive eye and head
Yield to duller lumps of lead,
When snaffling hand, and lying tongue,
And labyrinth gut, and bellows lung,
About the inhuman landscape spread
A natural history of the dead.

Shutting My Eyes

Shutting my eyes, I cannot see —
I can see no more
The tall walls, and the scud of the sea-spray
On the grey shale of the shore.

Shutting my ears, I cannot hear —
Or it lasts not long,
To drunken footsteps, the irreverent chorus
Of the drunken marching song.

Shutting my heart, I cannot feel —
But as a soft cloud
Shading the sun, the heart's branching ambition
By such dead foliage bowed.

Opening my eyes, I see too well
The daily task, the daily hell;
Opening my ears, I hear too loud
The sober nonsense of the crowd;
Opening my heart, I feel too weak
Towards the futile and the meek.

Open or shut, the eyes must see
What is, or can no longer be;
Open or shut, the ears must hear
A tale of folly or of fear:
Open or shut, the heart must know
How on the oak the ivies grow.

Shutting my eyes I long to see,
Shutting my ears I long to hear,
Some face that left no mask with me,
Some voice unechoed in my ear.

And when I come to shut my heart
I long to feel an old wound smart.

Shutting all these, I cannot shut,
No, not shut the mind
Still burning with the white weal of that beauty
That made ears deaf, eyes blind.

Pattern of History

Dialectic? The meeting of opposed faces,
In the narrow pass: the embrace closer than love's
And striding over the fallen body
In his fall you are encumbered:
His hands hold you, his will infects
Your simple conqueror's will. Goths, Normans,
Lombards, many a simple man: Attila:
But what survived was Rome, unbroken,
Building her straight roads now in the mind.

O Death, old captain, the wind is on the water:
The white sails of your yacht, and
The tall masts sloping. Anchor is up, and you
Off to your new country. The pitchy sea
And these adventurers alight with hope,
But doomed for drowning, drowning out of sounding,
Too deep for the voracious beaks of gulls.

Or if some scurvied and rebellious crew
Pass the great whirlpools and the monstrous whale,
What is their profit? A harsh foreshore,
Green rubber plants of jungle, paths to hack,
And when they reach the city they must kill:
O Death, old captain, your conquistadores,
Simple and noble, all intolerant Spain
In their contempt and cruelty; they are made
Means (we must believe it) for some new
Shape to work clumsily up to life;
Midwives for a dying mother. And they die, and
Even for us, far from the high seas,
Far from Montezuma's city,
In the long night the beak shall not spare hearts.

What shapes upon the clouds, the leaves of fancy,
Borne upon what winds? What men come riding,
What are these banners and these deathly cries?
Who lugged the gun to square the narrow bridge?
Who sniped from the high pine on the hillside?
These soldiers say, they have so long been marching,
They have forgotten destination and enemy.

The sea is black as ink, the roads are narrow,
And these sour fields make phosphate of our bones:
It is not seen that the hand did
What the mind would: monuments crumbled,
Honest utterance made rhetoric, poetry
Turning back in terror to the poet's mind.
And yet our eyes drink an inhuman brightness,
And yet our lips are gay with an illusion.

Black Flag

(from the French of Guy Rosey)

For the eye that is a flower of the fields
The iron-shelled day is an oyster
Just as through the winged presence of a landscape,
With red pom-poms, with red paps,
The feverish minutes violating the treaty
That the looks should be only at lace
Are the small lights of a happy homestead
At the edge of an unknown that can only weep:
There other loves raise up their walls
In the blue of inviolable memory,
The vaguely marvellous bird
That leads all the coaxing falseness of singing
To war at the foot of the rock.

Intuitive and carnivorous
Pool with the cry of a star that threads...

Prison painted on my face
Where the walls feel like four
Suffering more than its own life,
Like disfigured winter
Whose scars for it may be lovelier,
Like the idol
Raised upward by the colonising hand...

See, by the paths beaten by slow fevers,
The time of huge nocturnal mewing,
Of velvet, and of lucid incantations
Where man
Breaker of the dead and of their deeds
Scrapes the resisting gold
Full of noises like a virgin forest...

Crisis

My room as usual a disorder of books,
Nothing to my hand, my clothes flung on a chair,
My desk squalid and fussy with useless papers,
I had shut myself up from the clean shock of day.
I was asleep: like a criminal, without dreams.
There was nothing I desired but my own pride.

Then it seemed to me the earth opened,
I was on a green slope, an unsafe hillside,
With rocks there and rivers; there was that lady
And one man, my enemy. We three clung together
And rolled down the hill. The river whelmed,
I gripped her greedily. Then came sorrow,
She was not with me, I drowned alone:
That man mocked on the bank.

               I almost awakened,
But sorrow and sleep together bind fast.
Falling far, I came to a strange city,
No one knew me, I walked in sorrow alone.
Past smoke-black brick and yellow muslin curtains,
Vainly round interminable corners,
For these streets were familiar and not familiar
(The old tenements of Glasgow and my childhood)
And I knew I would never find my own house.

Then I met myself in my dream, I said clearly,
'I am going soon, take care of yourself, find friends.'
But my own eyes looked through me, my voice said, 'Traitor!'

And I saw then
All the terrible company of the defeated,
Lost but in the courage of shapes of stone:
The stone mouths of the rigid orators,
The elbow half-lifted in a thousand club-rooms
And the steady hand on the trigger turned to stone:
Then I awoke, sweating: I came out to the window,
In the evening light saw the snow grey on the ground.
I turned to my darkening room, I saw my papers
Scattered about, my life too lately
Had been all in bits. 'My God,' I said, 'there is something
Far wrong, certainly, somewhere. But with me or the world?'

Reasonings in a Dream

Constant and virtuous, whose hope lies deathwards
Beyond the raven and the hooded snake,
My lady lies dissected on your tables:
This total judgment of my grief I make,

This total judgment your analysis
Cannot destroy, your partial truths confute:
Sisters, who with the scalpel of the evening
Severed the link of angel and of brute.

Constant and virtuous, whose deathward signposts
Constrain my lady to that bloody lake
To lie among the common wreck of creatures:
This partial judgment of my grief I make,

For armed in silk, with pointed breasts for armour,
Or rather for their arms of attack,
These shadows have destroyed my soul's commander:
What fancy had, my grief must ever lack.

I with the grief of my too much unloving
Spilt the unjellied past upon the floor,
Setting the taint of meat among the gardens:
Furies, come back to harry me no more!

My love was lost in strife, my old affections
Desire of change to muffled fury turned:
I, who have neither love nor will to change now,
Hardly remember how my fancy burned,

Hardly remember all these toys and wonders:
What made the change or caused the sliding back:
I, lonely in my blessing and damnation,
Unfed desire, and undesiring lack.

Sonnet

My simple heart, bred in provincial tenderness,
And my cold mind, that takes the world for theme,
With local pain, with universal remedy,
Avert the real, disturb the noble dream:

And if my hand could touch you timidly,
Or I could laugh with you, and worry less
About the loud guns laughing over Europe,
I might find a local remedy, a province's hope:

Or if I had the hard steel mind of Lenin,
The skill or even the rage of Catiline
Against the corrupt, the comfortable. Then in

The pages of history one page might be mine.
But for my heart my mind must lose its scope,
And for my mind my heart must give up hope.

Elegy for Freud and Yeats

The sober and inquiring mind
And the enchanting charlatan
Moulded with tales and rhetoric
All that our age will or can,

Both at last found in the body's
Sweet imagined exercise
The pattern of the poet's metre
And the politician's lies.

Life for both was metaphor;
Towers for both as symbols stood,
Where the mind toiled up the round stair
Like the pulsing phallic blood,

Both forgave our sins, which were
But a strange and formal mask
For the familiar matter of
Every lover's nightly task.

Both saw in sexual ecstasy
The centre and the clue of all
Symbols, even geometry's
Cone and cylinder and ball.

Both, with this thought preoccupied,
Ignored the gathering general doom,
Whose belated thunders burst
Over either honoured tomb.

A Letter to Anne Ridler

A bird flies and I gum it to a concept,
You trim your concept to the flying bird,
Your round words plopping open out in rings.
May your love's dreams be innocent and absurd
For dreaming of your verses while he slept
You mastered these oblique and tricky things...

But I was a reporter on a paper
And saw death ticked out in a telegram
On grey and shabby sheets with pallid print
So often, that it seemed an evening dram
Of solace for the murderer and the raper
Whose love has grown monstrous through stint.

I was a poet of this century
Pursued by poster-strident images
And headlines as spectacular as a dream
Full of cartoonists' dolls with paper visages;
I had no spare time over for reality,
I took things largely to be what they seem.

I had a headache from the endless drum,
The orator drumming on his private anger,
And the starved young in their accusing group
When I had written and could write no longer
Over my shoulder seemed to peer and stoop.
The adequate perspectives would not come.

It was not real, the news I got from London,
But made the immediate avenue unreal
And sapped my habits of their privilege:
Dreamy the granite in the evening sun
And like a vision, in their swoop and wheel,
The pigeons fluttering at Union Bridge.

The Communists were always playing darts,
The Spanish War survivor would not talk,
The Tory member only talked of peace.
In spring, the ash-buds blossomed in our hearts,
The tangle blossomed on the slimy rock,
The private impulse sought its vain release...

And in December on the ballroom floor
The girls in flowering dresses swayed and whirled,
And no girl leant on my protective arm.
From all the height of speculation hurled,
I stood and hesitated by the door;
I felt the pathos and I felt the charm...

Oh, I had hardly any will or shape,
Or any motive, but a sort of guilt
That half attracted them and half repelled;
My hand shook, and my glass of sherry spilt,
I wore a sort of silence like a cape.
The old historic constant pattern held.

And when at midnight in my lonely room
I tried to integrate it all in verse
The headlines seemed as distant as the girls.
If sex was useless, history was worse.
A terrible remoteness seemed my doom
Whether I wrote of bayonets or curls...

So the stiff stanzas and the prosy lines
Accumulated on my dusty shelf,
A family joke, like any secret vice:
Dud bombs, damp rockets, unexploded mines.
'This sort of writing isn't really nice.
Oh, George, my darling, can't you be yourself?'

You can; and I would praise your studied art,
Dry and stiff-fingered, but more accurate
Than all my brilliant angers and my blind,
Hot, hurt perceptions, energised with hate:
Would praise your calm perspectives of the mind
So coloured with the pathos of the heart.

For my slack words were awkwardly herioc,
Your noble mood assumes no airs at all:
A rock of anger in this world unstable,
Me other people's sufferings made a stoic,
But you, a hostess, at our hungry table,
Are kind; your atmosphere is germinal.

Loving the charity of women's love,
Too much a household pet, I see in you
The gentle nurture that now curbs my grief
As I grow tall, beyond that budding grove
Of all the beautiful beyond belief
Within whose shade my windflower passions blew,

Private to me, their shy and secret sun:
Who now with other private suns compete
And seek in man's inverted mode such love

As nerves the will to enter and complete
Its terrible initiation of
Man to these virtues that from pain are won.

And the sick novice whimpers for his home
Who shall be hurt and horribly alone
Before the historic vigil lets him sleep.
Yet for such hurt, such pity might atone
And such an Ithaca for those who roam
Far, that they may at last return and weep.

Why do the towers of Troy for ever burn?
Perhaps that old Jew told us, or perhaps
Since women suffer much in bearing us
We also must show courage in our turn,
Among these forks and dreaded thunder-claps,
Against an endless dialectic tearing us…

Or freedom, say, from family love and strife
And all the female mystery of a room
That half supports and half imprisons us
May tear a man from mother, sister, wife,
And every soft reminder of the womb.
Dead Freud in lost Vienna argued thus.

I hardly know! But Fritz, who's now interned,
(Sober and well-informed like all his race)
Told me this war might last, say, seven years;
But right would be triumphant then, the tide be turned,
Unless indeed (the night fell on his face)
Our hopes are just illusions like our fears.

Perhaps in London, say, in seven years,
We'll meet, and we will talk of poetry,
And of the piety of homely things,
A common past, the flowering library
In which the awkward spirit perseveres
Until a world of letters shines and sings…

Unless the vigilant years have numbed my face,
The long humiliation soured my heart,
The madman's silence boxed my veering mood:
Let time forgive me, if I fall apart,
And fall, as many souls have fallen from grace,
Through just and necessary servitude.

Or if we never meet, remember me
As one voice speaking calmly in the north
Among the muslin veils of northern light;
I bore the seed of poetry from my birth
To flower in rocky ground, sporadically,
Until I sleep in the unlaurelled night.

Lament

Down by the drumming autumn of the river
Is a griever's evening, cracker of crazy leaves,
Is fire-snap, whip-snap, is bright weather dancing:
Is a swan-reft river, inconsolably grieves.

Is suave his image high from drowning river,
High from these nodding branches and green pools,
This swan, whom waters of my desolation
Would sully sky for, but this not consoles.

Would say these waters do like salt sea lap
For a smooth rock, that is ribs and is lips;
Is a salt-crusted autumn, with salt-crisp leaves
Are sea that crackles and loops and whips.

Say autumn and ocean, swan and rock, are all
But other truths for other images:
My swan or rock whom broke my truth against
I must pursue my water's truth, he says.

Now lap and ebb on this receding shore
Whose grains no grip have, nor no surging breast
For to arrest my tide or breast my river:
To me it was never given, ever, to have rest.

Poem for M.J.

These nervous and golden evenings, under the lamp
You will turn strict and pale to another smile,
And other hands will help you off with your coat,
And other voices will praise and qualify
Discussing a mood or a style
And raised as your sentences die with a jerk in your throat.
And outside at night it will be dark and damp
And against the raw damp sky
Your medallion will offer a scare to the sidling glance.
Oh, perhaps in some house you pass there will be music,
Perhaps people will dance.

Here I am soothed by the sad, the satiable sea,
Here I ride with a trident the blue imperial wave,
Here I am drowned by the hands, voices, and faces
That move, sound, and behave,
Here I am smiling to think it is not you,
My dear, or your sort that intermit the wars
To root us from our vegetating places,

It's not for you the towers of Troy shall burn;
But you are like that patient Ithaca
To which, from all the headaches of the sea,
After ten years of labouring at the oars,
Some few, the luckier voyagers, return.

A Letter to Nicholas Moore

So few are lucky in the natural mode
And I was always an unlucky one,
With greed's shy gaze for the expensive treat
Of beauty, excellent in bone and blood,
Responsive to the same considering sun
That soured the grapes I never dared to eat.

Mine was the bitter gaze to pore upon
A profile or the modelling of an ear
Or the dry waxy pallor of two hands.
Mine was the pillow for the midnight tear
For all the deeds which could not be undone
And all the seeds wherewith I'd sown the sands.

Mine was the coward's humble insolence
That warms itself at an unheeding fire
And writes a poem to the kindly blaze,
Mine was the nibbling mouth without defence
Against the hook of any stray desire
That fractured the dead water of my days...

And thus, incompetent to speak of love,
I learned affection's humbler discipline,
And could be plain and easy with my friends
But yet stood still, where suns and planets move
Through love that turns their ellipses in,
For I had not their purposes and ends...

Or if I had, my density was such
That as another's star I could not move
Or I was tied to black and secret suns,
Lost memories, that held my heart too much,
A child's desire for universal love,
Or some blind, blank devotion like the nun's,

Or my own face in someone's flattering glass
That now my hateful mirror would not show,
Fixed to a pallor with a squinting eye,
Sir Death, expectant in the narrow pass,
A lame explorer nursing wastes of snow
That in his summer nightmares flower and die,

Or say, like that diseased great Baudelaire,
Sipping his small black coffee in the sun
And licking with his tongue at rotting teeth
And keeping up a poised and public air
While at his skull the endless headaches dun,
And round his cane imagined worms wreath.

I was the man, for poetry and not love,
To whom disaster is a kind of show,
His mind an emblem of the shattering world.
A pose? I could not hold it, say! I move
From that high tower of private pathos hurled
On the same street where all the others go,

But if I love, my love is general.
To all suns tied, but not to any sun;
My mind is still an emblem, but of man
Weary at midday, but still standing tall
To do whatever he has left undone,
And then at night to find what peace he can...

There's still a kind of headache, there is still
A sort of setness in my walk and air,
There's still sad hunger on my lonely lips.
There's still the lonely poised considering will
Watching those faces with their floating hair
That pass from my horizon, like lost ships.

All this is egoism, as I know.
Let me be sane and sensible and flat.
Perhaps the healthy impulse will persist,
Although it interrupts the lyric flow.
All I have written might boil down to that —
Well, nobody can love an egoist!

But you, my friend, I think, were always loved,
Were always lucky in the natural mode
And now your luck has turned to certainty:
That was the impulse by which I was moved
Before the horse ran that I thought I rode —
To offer flowers to your felicity.

Lord, what a growler at a marriage feast!
The grunts of a disgruntled bachelor,
The envy of a wintry old maid!
Accept our conscious courtesy at least
Now we remember what the gathering's for
And feel compunction for the parts we've played.

May you know all love's honey-sweet delights,
May all your friends be happy as I am
That new enrichment brings your gifts increase.

May you walk happy on these summer nights
By dappled willows on the quiet Cam
And may the warm arches bless your peace.

Home Town Elegy

(For Aberdeen in Spring)

Glitter of mica at the windy corners,
Tar in the nostrils, under blue lamps budding
Like bubbles of glass the blue buds of a tree,
Night-shining shopfronts, or the sleek sun flooding
The broad abundant dying sprawl of the Dee:
For these and for their like my thoughts are mourners
That yet shall stand, though I come home no more,
Gas-works, white ballroom, and the red brick baths
And salmon nets along a mile of shore,
Or beyond the municipal golf-course, the moorland paths
And the country lying quiet and full of farms.
This is the shape of a land that outlasts a strategy
And is not to be taken with rhetoric or arms.
Or my own room, with a dozen books on the bed
(Too late, still musing what I mused, I lie
And read too lovingly what I have read),
Brantome, Spinoza, Yeats, the bawdy and wise,
Continuing their interminable debate,
With no conclusion, they conclude too late,
When their wisdom has fallen like a grey pall on my eyes.
Syne we maun part, their sall be nane remeid —
Unless my country is my pride, indeed,
Or I can make my town that homely fame
That Byron has, from boys in Carden Place,
Struggling home with books to midday dinner,
For whom he is not the romantic sinner,
The careless writer, the tormented face,
The hectoring bully or the noble fool,
But, just like Gordon or like Keith, a name:
A tall, proud statue at the Grammar School.

Nilotic Elegy

Sometimes I seemed to see gliding the green
Ghost of a landscape, sometimes other summers
Were marginal upon the summer scene,
Sometimes the river's waft was wet with rumours
Of other scents, the tingle of the sea,
Sometimes the passing walker was the echo
Of one who waits on other shores for me,

Sometimes the sliding mask of the felucca
Spoke of enchanted summer voyages
Through rhododendrons or past shining bathers
To all my lost imaginary Venuses:
Sometimes these thoughts would have their doubtful sharers,
Sniffing the odours of a greensick youth
That spilt its promise on the soils of fancy
And in the rose and tulip found its truth.
Sometimes I thought how broken and how chancy
The tides of every sexual river are
That make the sandy valleys black and fertile
To crop a maggot summer of despair.
But yet I weave the rue and yet the myrtle,
But yet I weave the laurel, and I find
Still stained with a green magic from the south,
Weeds of a boy's desire, my Theban flood.
O walls of Karnac, buttress in your blind!
From the high sources to the stammering mouth
I chose the sun and every chance of blood...

To His Brother's Spirit

(from Catullus)

Far by innumerable folk, far by the sea far carried,
To these sad obsequies, O my brother, I come;

I come to offer you the extreme donation of death
And to pay my debts to a mute ash in an urn,

Since from my love thee, thee Fortune hath snatched,
Thee with cruel harshness, O unfortunate brother!

Pure gold these gifts to thy sad rites I've carried,
As the ancient custom is: as pure gold, take them.

Take these gifts with a brother's tears still dripping:
And my brother, good-bye, and good-bye, and again, and for ever!

The Fountain of Bandusia

(from Horace)

To thee I gave a limpid glass, most limpid,
Worthy of ambrosial vintage and of flowery
Garlands, and will to-morrow give,
O fountain of Bandusia,

A youngling kid, one from whose swelling
Forehead the tenuous horns sprout already
    Almost ripe for amorous
    And for rougher battles,

Who with his vermeil blood will tinge,
Fountains, thy fresh and freezing streams;
    To-morrow, this firstling fruit
    Of the lascivious herd.

You give to the ox weary from the ploughshare
And to the flocks delightful freshness freely:
    O may the hateful burning
    Of the sun not consume thee,

Thee noble among fountains, if I praise
In song the erect ilex and the concave
    Pebbles where on their voluble way
    Your pure waters are flowing.

To Pyrrha

(from Horace)

Pyrrha, what graceful boy now to your rosy
Couch besprinkled with liquid odours
    Under your cave are you tying?
    For whom sprucely, but simply

Curls that gold head?...Ah, how many tear-drops
For that too volatile heart of yours he'll be shedding
    And for the changed Fates!
    Like as the waves unstable

I admire astonished him who still credulous
Takes joy in you as golden pure, and amiable,
    Hopes so to prove you ever,
    Of winds' misfaith unwitting!

But O what grief will blast him unawares!
Already my dank garments with a votive
    Tablet upon the holy wall
    I've hung up to the ruler of the sea...

Rostov

That year they fought in the snow
On the enormous plain, the rivulets
Thick with the yellow thaw, and darker, dark
With what at distance might be blood or shadows:
Everything melted, everything numbed, broke,
Every hand was pawing at desolation
And the huge, stupid machine felt a shudder.
It did not matter about all the dead
For what better than death in battle
(The sick voice said in the belly,
'What better than death in battle?')
And the heart had been numbed long ago
Against particular pity (yes, and some,
And some have had their pact against all pity:
'If we ask mercy, let it be counted weakness,
And if we repent, let it be counted strategy!')

But the artillery in its tremendous
Asseveration of another existence
Was like the mask of Lenin, thundering power
From a controlled centre. And lumbering
Came the great new tanks, and always
The artillery kept saying, 'You make
An effort but it exhausts itself,
Everything meets its shock.' And some
Seemed to hear in its thunder, just
The syllables of that strong man, 'They want
A war of extermination, let them have it!'
And there was always blinding and stupefying
The snow, the wet, the shivering soddenness:
And a purpose against one roused that meant death.

So the thing began to stagger, lumbering back,
Reeling under these statements, propositions,
The oratory of the last argument death:
Hammering, hammering, hammering home,
'One man is like another, one strength
Like another strength, and the wicked
Shall not prosper for ever, and the turns
Of history bring the innocent to victory;'
The guns lashing like Churchill's sentences
Or the blows of a whip.
            The terrible strength of Tolstoy,
And Dostoevsky's vision, Lenin's silences,
The great, crude, broad-thewed man with innocent eye
Standing like a queer rock in the path:
And lashing death like lightnings from the heavens.

That year it had rained death like apples,
That year the wicked were strong. But remember
That the time comes when the thing that you strike
Rouses itself, suddenly, very terribly,
And stands staring with a terribly patient look
And says, 'Why do you strike me brother? I am Man.'

Lament

In a dismal air; a light of breaking summer
Under the conspicuous dolour of a leaden sky,
We walk up by the river, beneath the deciduous branches;
Cold in the water the webs of the cold light lie.

Always the sky bleeds with sorrow that no light stanches
In the evenings of autumn, when rust coloured crisp leaves fly.
Always the heart is uneasy and full of foreboding:
Always the heart is uneasy and cannot tell why.

Always the rust of the leaves and the light is corroding
The steel of the evening, gun-metal blue of the sky.
Always the river is lisping and lapping of sorrow.
Like the leaves and the light, the incontinent impulses die.

No more appointments to meet and continue tomorrow,
No more postponements of parting, with hesitant sigh,
Here's the great year in its circle, announcing departure.
Here are your hard lips on mine and good-bye and good-bye.

Summer resumes the occasion but not the adventure.
Always the heart is uneasy and cannot tell why.
In a dismal air; a light of breaking summer,
Cold in the water the webs of the cold light lie.

Christmas Letter Home

(To my sister in Aberdeen)

Drifting and innocent and sad like snow,
Now memories tease me, wherever I go,
And I think of the glitter of granite and distances
And against the blue air the lovely and bare trees,
And slippery pavements spangled with delight
Under the needles of a winter's night,
And I remember the dances, with scarf and cane,
Strolling home in the cold with the silly refrain
Of a tune of Cole Porter or Irving Berlin
Warming a naughty memory up like gin,

And Bunny and Sheila and Joyce and Rosemary
Chattering on sofas or preparing tea,
With their delicate voices and their small white hands
This is the sorrow everyone understands.
More than Rostov's artillery, more than the planes
Skirting the cyclonic islands, this remains,
The little, lovely taste of youth we had:
The guns and not our silliness were mad,
All the unloved and ugly seeking power
Were mad, and not our trivial evening hour
Of swirling taffetas and muslin girls,
Oh, not their hands, their profiles, or their curls,
Oh, not the evenings of coffee and sherry and snow,
Oh, not the music. Let us rise and go —
But then the months and oceans lie between,
And once again the dust of spring, the green
Bright beaks of buds upon the poplar trees,
And summer's strawberries, and autumn's ease,
And all the marble gestures of the dead,
Before my eyes caress against your head,
Your tiny strawberry mouth, your bell of hair,
Your blue eyes with their deep and shallow stare,
Before your hand upon my arm can still
The nerves that everything but home makes ill:
In this historic poster-world I move,
Noise, movement, emptiness, but never love.
Yet all this grief we had to have my dear,
And most who grieve have never known, I fear,
The lucky streak for which we die and live,
And to the luckless must the lucky give
All trust, all energy, whatever lies
Under the anger of democracies:
Whatever strikes the towering torturer down,
Whatever can outface the bully's frown,
Talk to the stammerer, spare a cigarette
For tramps at midnight...oh, defend it yet!
Some Christmas I shall meet you. Oh, and then
Though all the boys you used to like are men,
Though all my girls are married, though my verse
Has pretty steadily been growing worse,
We shall be happy: we shall smile and say,
'These years! It only seems like yesterday
I saw you sitting in that very chair.'
'You have not changed the way you do your hair.'
'These years were painful, then?' 'I hardly know.
Something lies gently over them, like snow,
A sort of numbing white forgetfulness...'

And so, good-night, this Christmas, and God bless!

The Traveller has Regrets

1948

The Traveller has Regrets was first published by the Harvill Press in 1948.

The Traveller has Regrets

The traveller has regrets
For the receding shore
That with its many nets
Has caught, not to restore,
The white lights in the bay,
The blue lights on the hill,
Though night with many stars
May travel with him still,
But night has nought to say,
Only a colour and shape
Changing like cloth shaking,
A dancer with a cape
Whose dance is heart-breaking,
Night with its many stars
Can warn travellers
There's only time to kill
And nothing much to say:
But the blue lights on the hill,
The white lights in the bay
Told us the meal was laid
And that the bed was made
And that we could not stay.

The Absence of the Dead

Long and composed, upon
A narrow lap, her hands
Rise at a bait and fly,
Impinging on no air:
Watch them to understand
Her harsh beguiling eye,
As still and swift as these,
Watch what is dead and gone,
Delusive images...
Long at this nothing stare.

All these phenomena were
Imprinted on a body that
Thick strife has swallowed:
Without it, are not her.
Projected, but not flat,
These make a deep impress,
These carve a sad no-sense,
A void round and hollowed.
Bake, Void, with Fire she had
Whom Earth has taught patience:
Water, be still and sad:
Air, be this emptiness.
All elements are mad.

We, in the dead of night,
Caught in our own surprise
Have heard our own breath
Move in a beast's gasp,
Grasping at us, would grasp
Hots, Colds, Wets, Dries,
Knowing unravelling Death:
Who calls this knowledge slight?

Though its matter is spent,
Thought sustains elegance:
Seen in a fretful year,
On a conversational day,
Elaborate discontent
With her frangible matter
Making that form clear
That it would waste away.
In the corner where she sat,
Nursing her long beer,
With her insolent hat,
Dust and the sun now dance.

Grief is as vain as rage.
Certain acquaintances please
And certain doors close
Quietly, with no clatter.
Time, that can discompose
Material certainties,
Has discomposed this image.

The Death of My Grandmother

There's little personal grief in a quiet old death:
Grief for a landscape dying in our heads,
Knowing how London melts us to her style.
What if she got those touches in her talk
(The half-impression of a scene that had
Flowed in her youthful blood and set as bone)
From phrases in some novel by John Buchan?
A memory is other than the words for it:
Persistence was her gift, not literature,
A character no town could penetrate,
Not Glasgow's sprawl, nor London's repetitions —
No more that landscape now: no more the old
Books in the glass case, and the box bed
I half remember as a boy in Glasgow:
Caithness enclosed within a house in Glasgow,
Glasgow enclosed in London: time in time,
The past within the past, parentheses.
In laying her to rest, it is as if
We folded up with her brown age a landscape,
A ribbed and flat and rocky map of duty
That is the northern edge of every island
Where pleasure flowers only in the swollen south:
Mourn character that could persist so long
Where softer personality dies young.

These lights and glimpses lost now: only bones,
Shapes of our heads, only the arguing voice,
In a foreign milieu the improvised fine manners.

Think of these rock-stacks in the stony Orkneys
That, toppling, stand improbably for years,
The sea persisting at them: and at last,
Boys' bricks, they crash on the untidy beach.
So with her piled and uncemented past:
Its tottering tower seemed out of the tide's reach.
Time merely fretted at the base. No more
Of all the colour of her years was hers
Than brown rock's is blue sea's. O travellers,
Who take the stain of Time, as I have done,
Expose your fluctuations to the sun:
Yet, for such stony virtue, spare your tears.

Three Poems about Love

I

Here I stand at the bar
Sipping with bitter relish
The brandy dregs of an evening
That morning will embellish

With the prestige of the lost
Chance, of the easy charms
Slipped from my slack fingers
Into my good friend's arms.

O flower fallen in the water,
O love lost like a leaf,
O golden cargo, gone to wrack
Upon my shores of grief,

Drinking, as often before
Of a cup prepared too often,
I think again of these things
Which no thinking will soften:

The abstruse clues that I had,
The obvious ones that I lacked,
And the recurrent mystery:
No image is intact.

II

For the faces discompose
And the letters disconnect
And desire's murderous rage
Has an opiate effect,

So that the face of Mary
Blends with Maria's face
And the possible situation
Recurs in any place.

I shall coax some other woman
Into a yielding mood:
But then if rage and jealousy
Return in their flood

And the woman easy to me
Be easy to other men?
Knowing the end in the start
Shall I suffer this again?

Or like slow fuses burning
Towards the shrapnel case
Shall my stored furies shatter
Love from an innocent face?

Then, the terrific explosion:
All our façades cracked:
Ruin made by my folly:
And no image intact?

III

All that I got from love
Was the impulse to write
Verse for my own and others'
But seldom her delight,

Her whom my verse transforms
As the plain image in time
Loses particular presence
In the tapestry of rhyme,

That flowing tapestry
Where, mingled like a stream,
All possible delights
And lost fulfilments gleam:

And time transforms her, too,
And all her light would die
But for this echo, this effect,
This agonising cry.

What image is intact
From all that brilliant crowd
But those that wrung my heart
And made me cry aloud?

Flemish Primitive

Soft petals fell out of a brooding air
Like blossoms of the apple or the pear,

Soft magic, like the feathers of a dove,
Fell on this lady and her little love.

Up in the inn, the travellers sat to dine,
Pouring hot spices in their steaming wine.

Out on the street, the sentry stamped and swore,
Knowing his guard must last for one hour more.

The Three Wise Kings were on their homeward road,
Their hearts unburdened of the ruler's load,

While Herod slept; but, dreaming of disaster,
He felt his heart, that nightmare, beat the faster.

Back on the hill, a Shepherd scratched his head
To find the sense of what the Angels said.

But in her dark Byzantine green and gold,
This sleeping miracle repelled the cold.

The green was fodder, and the gold was straw;
But Mary sang a lullaby and saw

Azure and gilt around her; the intense
And choking fragrance of the frankincense

Swirled in her dream. A thought of stillness was
Sick longing in her soul. She wished to pause

From thought, from movement, and from grief; to rest
For ever with her baby at her breast.

Good Friday, 1945

... the loss of Time is more,
The loss of Christ is such a loss
As no man can restore.

And I have felt *Time's* loss
As from my thirtieth year
I turned and looked across
Words. I have felt the fear
As in a tarnished glass
To find no image clear
Of what was real, alas!
Where is lean *Love* beside
His autumn river? Pass,
Dream, what the day denied.
Let a windy night return
With his strong hands to hide
My trembling hand. Or burn
In the brown glass these leaves
In which the years return,
For also this deceives:
Deceptive is the dream
That gives and that bereaves
The falling leaves, the stream,
And twirls the *Past* away
Towards a darker theme.

One said, the *Past* will stay:
It sits and it will sit
Untouched by our decay.
I know we alter it
And that in *Dante's Hell*
Where in the tombs they sit
It never has been well,
There are no gardens there
With their autumnal smell
Though these have been. The hair
Of *Thais* has smelled sweet
But smells no longer there
Except of charring heat.
We trample all the *Past*
With our strong bruising feet.
And nothing gone will last
Except as consequence
And molten metal cast
In final bronze: and thence,
From that last brazen hour,
Who plucks lost *Innocence*?

The *Good* lay in our power:
But in this sulphur land
What but the wire can flower
And to the writhing hand
What has the coal restored?
Do any fruit-trees stand
Against these banks abhorred
By the steel rain? What *Love*
Can wade the bitter ford?

And in some sphere above
Choice, with what irony,
What bright *Potentials* move!

To the Death that is the Muse of Adolescence

When I was young and summer easier,
Famous beauty, I traced your admired features
In a fair summer profile, a medal in gold
Whose pride would never deign to look at me.

Your exploits were those, also, of the dashing
Brown and muscular, of the taciturn
Athletes. The life in my own feebleness
Beat feebly against that bronze impression.

I admired so much beauty and strength, all
Serving you, going down your unspoken ways,
These beauties whose only laurel was my look,
These marchers stepping to a final frontier.

But, Death, you knew me a poet! Admiration
Was all you sought, intruding into my dream:
You were the drooping willows, the calm swans,
The stream, the wooded path that led nowhere.

And now I can see your obvious deception:
That you let the curtain down, but are not the play,
That you limit our chances, but are not among them.
You are no more than the outer edge of the poem.

And those I admired as terribly dedicated
To you, were in fact those in whom their lives
Had terribly taken form, and what I admired
Was not a thing you knew about or could hinder:

Perhaps you are the general condition, perhaps
Life tends to shapeless sag, vain repetition,
Average life not very different from death—
But formal beauty or strength always astonishing.

Therefore if I see you now it is as a shapeless
Amiable acquaintance, pouched eyes in the tube,
Shrugged shoulders in the pub, humorous whining:
'It's beyond me, chum... Well, what could I do'?

For in myself and others you are the wish
To give up trying, to throw in the hand,
To be quite free from all demands upon one:
On my living face I know you as a sullen stare.

I am aware of you not, indeed, with hostility
But with a certain distaste, as at flabby muscles,
A drooling tongue, a refusal to concentrate:
As a certain negative interpenetration

Touching the taste of life with padded wool,
Soaking the blood up, making the pain nothing:
As the anaesthesia of those who are very tired,
And who fiddle about with their hands, and shape nothing;

As sentences written or spoken falling flat,
As a hollow note in the ear, an attempt to grasp
Through a blank eye at a meaning that merely crumbles:
As the pathos of an old woman in the park,

Sitting on a bench, in black, surrounded by parcels,
Her veiny hands gripping an old umbrella,
A thick scarf winding her parroty neck,
And a tear...a glacial tear...in her rheumy eye.

That is the pathos of life and death, the pathos
Of the live tear in her dying poor old eye!
The helpless unlovely thing whose pain breeds pity.
There, not war, is your true domain as an artist,

Though even there the real pathos is life,
Life that feels itself dying, feels the cold.
Your triumph as a philistine to quiet that feeling:
As an artist, to leave it just a little alive!

Without this concept of the shapeless, no shape:
Without your gulf at the edge, no edge to living!
But I shall not be lyrical now about *your* prestige...
I have felt the taste of nothing on my own tongue.

Tablet in Memory

You, who have forgotten me completely now, remain
A durable image, standing like a column
Whose marble from the storm-winds takes no stain;
Tall, like Athene, straight, and white, and solemn,
You vanish last in the dismembering night
That flays and opens all the good and fair;
You are the morning, very cold and white;
You are the room for which I climb the stair.
You are the lucid and forgiving page
That lends a shiftless history point and order;
You are the challenge and the noble rage;
You are the happy land across the border.
You are these dreams, but of your dreams not one
Is this hurt creature you took pity on.

The Black Cherub

Per la contradizione che nol consente
        Dante

Because the contradiction does not allow
Us to be happy and also to know how
I will give a penny to anyone who begs
And say my prayers at night to a girl's legs,

Because the contradiction does not consent
That what we say resemble what we meant
My sonnets perish in a burning shower,
My prose preserves the balance of the power,

Because the contradiction thinks it well
That casuists on the whole should go to hell
I shall balance revolution against heaven
And die a bourgeois still, and still unshriven,

Because the contradiction does not permit
Hegels to find a resolution for it
Hitlers who seek to unify the world
Shall be in the southernmost flames of hell curled,

With all the other fraudulent counsellors
Who tell the wicked how to cast down towers,
Who sell for gold the city or the girl,
And for whom now hell's horrid bagpipes skirl,

For they all go down to the teeth and the claws and the ice
Where Judas and Brutus realise they are not nice,
And the great poets wander and sniff from high
At the smell of hell's ineffable *canaille,*

And the only lucky are like Uberto who
Thought that they knew more than they really knew,
And who swell up erect from their bed of night,
'As if they held the Inferno in great despite,'

Or the scholarly old homosexual who still
Retains a pride in his grammatical skill
And though he must dodge the column, and cannot choose,
'Runs like the sprinters who win, and not who lose.'

Since our pride is not from God, by our own will
We can keep ourselves from the filthiest pouches still:
From the lake of pitch where the devils bite like curs
Or the sea of filth that engulfs the flatterers,

But at night we may go down on our cold knees:
'To-morrow, God, make me not a drunkard, please:
But let me have the pleasure of being drunk,'
And the contradiction has us, and we are sunk,

Or, 'Let my love be pure and gentle at last:
And let it be cleansed from the stains and the pains of the past:
And let the girl come easily to my bed,'
And the black cherub holds the hairs of our head.

But worse than us the hypocrites who cry,
'Let the world have peace, and let the starving die:
Let the rich lie in an easy bed at nights:
Let the fat dog sleep whom the wicked flea bites,

'O, let us have peace and let the heart be still:
The cold and the empty of heart will never kill:
Let the poor know how strong are the bars of the cage
That they may not shake them in their futile rage!'

For from love alone, and not from the cold grease
Of your rich tables, will you build peace,
Nor with your poverty constrain God's plenty:
Per la contradizione che nol consente!

A Lady asks Me

*(An attempt at the skeletonic sense – far from my scope, alas, the
supple outward glow – of 'Donna mi prega', Guido Cavalcanti's
famous poem on the nature of love.)*

A lady asks me: so I wish to speak
Of an inherent, often mettlesome,
That should be haughty, for its name is Love:
If she, denying Love, can feel Love truly!

And at this time I seek the man who knows,
Having no hope that any of base heart
To this high argument can raise his wits:
And, without prior demonstration, I,
Lacking the talent, lack the wish to prove
Where Love's seat is, and who created Love,
What is Love's virtue, what its potency,
Its essence, and its many moving acts,
And that delight that gives the name of Love:
And if a man can show Love to be seen.

In that same part where sits the Memory
Love takes its seat, so given its form as
Transparency from light, by an obscure
Influence from Mars, and among us makes stay.

Love is created, sentient, has a name,
From the soul vesture, from the heart a will,
And rises from a form, both seen and grasped,
That takes within the mind's potentiality,
As in its medium, proper place and dwelling.

Such form in such a place has never grief,
Since from its quality it cannot fall,
Shines in its own effect perpetually:
It is to contemplate, not to enjoy,
So has no proper outward analogue.

Love is not virtue, but from that it comes
Which is perfection, claiming to be so,
Not rational...but which is felt, I say!
Love keeps the judgement from its saner rule
Because desire in reason's place prevails
And ill discerns in whom is vice a friend.
Love is not properly opposed to nature,
Yet from Love's sway there follows often death
So powerfully that virtue is impeded
Which helps us forward on the living road:
Yet just as he, who turns from perfect good
By chance, we cannot say that he has life,
Just so it is when a man forgets Love.

Love's essence is when the desire is such
That out of nature's cup it overflows
And takes no more adornment of repose.
Love moves, changing colour, laughter, and tears,
And all the face distorts with fears:
Is volatile: this, too, I scan,
Love's greatest strength is in the valorous man.

This novel quality moves sighs,
Nor wishes man should turn to a fixed place
(Who has not felt cannot imagine this:
There lurks its wrath, which wrath sends fires!)
Nor move, however drawn, to such a place,
Nor veer towards it, there to find his joy:
Small matter if the man be fool or wise!
Nor are the stubborn beauties Love's true dart,
Since such desire, for fear, will soon be spent:
Only the wounded spirit has the prize.

Love is not known by the face's aspect:
Already pale, the sick become its thrall:
Form, as the wise know, is not visible,
Therefore Love less, with Form as its cause:
Empty of colour and from being sundered,
Amidst obscurity sends out its rays!

Free from all fraud, a man worthy of faith
May say that such alone will give him grace.

You may go freely, now, my song,
Where'er you please. I have adorned you so
That many praises will your reasonings have
From all such persons as have understanding:
To please the rest my talent never was.

To a Scottish Poet

Goddess or ghost, you say, by shuddering,
    And ominous of evil to our land,
Twisting to ugliness the mouths that sing,
    Parching the lover's moist and balmy hand,

Goddess or ghost, you say, by silence known,
    The silence ticking in the rotten wood
Like our numb pain, that can no longer groan:
    A grief so old, it gives the mind no food.

I also on bleak nights in Causewayend
    Where the slate sky distorts the slaty stone
And the shawled women to their burrows wend,
    Have felt my country suffering alone.

The slate sea splashes on the slaty pier
    In lost St Andrews, where no poets now
Defy the crocodile to shed its tear
    Or take what time the bitter years allow.

And the same sea is loud in Aberdeen:
    Passing the gas-works and the fish-and-chips
One comes in summer on the radiant scene,
    The golden beach, the girls with golden hips,

The sun that cooks and savours all their sex:
    Then I have thought my country might arise
Like these half-sleeping girls with tawny necks
    And summer's sensual softness in their eyes.

These skies bled warmth: and while my blood stays young,
    That starving peace, or this protracted war,
Vows broken, or friends lost, or songs unsung
    Shall leave no permanent and vexing scar.

Goddess or ghost, you say, by shuddering,
    And ominous of evil to our land...
I say, defy her, while our blood can sing;
    While we stand insolent, as poets stand.

Epistle to an Unhappy Friend [2]

(Chelsea, February, 1946)

Look, dear, at my window now
A little snow falls slantingly,
Black dirt has daubed the red brick wall,
And invisible snowflakes fall
Beyond the dumb and shrinking trees
(Heart, poor heart, is black as these)
Among streaked pillars and the low
Sad gravestones in the cemetery:

Beyond that green of graves a square
Of houses closes my thinking in
And from that smeary sky the snow
Falls, as I watch, more flock-like. So
Indefinite and so sinister
On the shaped world in this false winter
There is blind fear in its white glare
And a softness sharper than a pin.

Yet, as I write, some impudent bird
Begins to chirrup and to quarrel
With the bricks of Chelsea, the drab snow,
Though I am dead at finger and toe
And would wish him silent, that I might be
A dumb brute in my misery
Without having to be made absurd
By his cheap pipe and his trite moral.

I am him to you. There is little I can
Do at this season, little at all,
Except to chirp with a half sigh
Winter will finish by and by
And then another month will bring
Our shabby sort of London spring...
(O shallow, tedious, kind young man!
Bright sparrow with your silly bawl!)

Egypt

Who knows the lights at last, who knows the cities
And the unloving hands upon the thighs
Would yet return to seek his home-town pretties
For the shy finger-tips and sidelong eyes.

Who knows the world, the flesh, the compromises
Would go back to the theory in the book:
Who knows the place the poster advertises
Back to the poster for another look.

But nets the fellah spreads beside the river
Where the green waters criss-cross in the sun
End certain migratory hopes for ever:
In that white light, all shadows are undone.

The desert slays. But safe from Allah's justice
Where the broad river of His Mercy lies,
Where ground for labour, or where scope for lust is,
The crooked and tall and cunning cities rise.

The green Nile irrigates a barren region,
All the coarse palms are ankle-deep in sand:
No love roots deep, though easy loves are legion:
The heart's as hot and hungry as the hand.

In airless evenings, at the café table,
The soldier sips his thick sweet coffee up:
The dry grounds, like the moral to my fable,
Are bitter at the bottom of the cup.

Exile's Letter

Exiled too long, my dear, I build
The dream by which the story's killed,
For if, in days of pride and glory,
The dream illuminates the story,
In days when things are what they seem
The story merely feeds the dream.
Exiled from you, what should I see?
A white hand on a wavering knee,
A sentence from a letter that
Is sly, and elegant, and pat,
A vista from a window where
The paths are brown, the trees are bare
(The dove-grey skies of evening laid
Across the olive shrub-choked glade)
And your white hand by wavering knee
Still offering buns, still pouring tea...
Tea done, what miry ways we walked
And what pedantic stuff we talked
(Abstruse, portentous, and oblique:
So shy and lettered lovers speak
And paused upon the stony brink
Too nicely feel, too vaguely think,

Peck, fumble, offer cigarettes,
Dive deep, and drown with choked regrets)
While waiting for the rumbling bus,
By continents dividing us:
But each sharp image I recall
Seems not to link with you at all,
A blank oppression clamps my mind,
At one sour sentence staring, blind,
The tritest thought that twists love's faith:
How time and distance *are* like death!

For...sift, select, refine the past,
As if each letter were the last,
Yet when another letter comes
On a less vivid ear it drums
And more at random one must talk
To make the speaking phantoms walk,
These ghosts whom time and distance chase
Across a similar poise or face
As Jean, who turns her lion's head
Across a Cairo street, misread,
Or Tom whom in an hour of dearth
I sought in living ghosts in Perth:
Many the narrow shoulders had,
The noble air, though slightly mad,
Many the bush of burning hair,
But the whole picture was not there:
And so for fragments some will please,
The eye to coax, the voice to tease,
The new chase out the old at last:
The present love digests the past.
The curse! that exiles settle down
At home in the barbarian town
And learn the local dialect too
(Like Pontic Ovid or Scotch you)
And never truly more at home
Than when they sigh, 'Remember Rome!'
Could I return to London's streets,
Or weather Scotland's winter sleets,
Another past would rise to slay:
Nostalgia in a Greek café,
The camel-dust of Cairo's night,
And the last stub I'd left to light —
Regrets for our regrets we'll prove,
And can it be the same with love? —
That he and she are both content
With what they *hope* the other meant,
With what a memory refines
When with a confidant one dines
And, swearing this liqueur the last,
Smacking the lips, declaims — 'The Past!'

But if the Past could present stand
With the raw nail-marks in Its hand
We'd wish It in the night outside
And fear to feel Its murdered side...

And you would say our whole age is
Exiled from the realities
And man, by nature exiled, must
Traverse the flaring streets of lust
To the dull barracks of his mind
If man is obdurately blind.
But all that I am sure of is
The exile's way is history's:
The old are exiled from the young,
I from the songs my body sung
When basking by the summer shore
I thought and dreamt and wished no more
Except to lie a summer long
With all the summer for my song:
I'm exiled from the studious boy
With books and gardens for his toy
Whose attic-window in its cup
Tilted the wine-dark evening up.
So exiled from ourselves we live
And yet can learn to forgive
The past that promised us so much
And ends, alas, my dear, in such,
Such chatter in an exile's town:
Such towers so tall, so tumbledown,
Such shabby places as we find
To sleep in and pull down the blind
And think, 'At last I am alone,
With no more failures to atone!'
A state — all exiles know it well —
Some call content; some, sloth; some, hell...

My dear, I write, as exiles will,
Half to revive and half to kill:
Revive the hope, and kill the ache:
Revive the promises we make
Crying before we go to sleep
And wake refreshed and do not keep.
I write it all at too much length,
To show my weakness is my strength,
And with no art, and yet to move,
To show my coldness is my love:
I write it all, and with a sigh
I'd write — no exile writes — good-bye.
No drowning man gives up a straw,
No ruined litigant the law,
No scribbler his scribbler's itch,
No needle's eye its struggling rich,

No exile his decaying dream,
No semblance what it used to seem,
No love its image of delight...
My dear, write soon. God bless. Good night.

A Native Girl in Decamere

She in her straight transparent muslin swayed
Like water in a glass. The brittle light
Upon the plum bloom of her body played;
And the mimosa tree was twice her height
That scattered yellow pollen at her feet.
All the clock faces told a different hour,
Only the hens were scratching in the street,
And in the sun she opened like a flower.
Like water in a glass, my thought was swirled
A moment by the garden and the door:
Then I climbed up to where the shite-hawks whirled
With kitten cries above the plateau floor,
And where the snaky, slaty road wound down
To sting, with lecherous fang, the sleepy town.

Epistle to J.G. [3]

(Cairo, October 1944)

'That I might live in these quiet forests
And write with integrity,'
Wrote Maynard once, whose interests
Were of a poverty

No doubt extreme, compared
To his who sees
The stone forests of Europe bared
Of glass leaves, the trees,

The mind's trees, stripped of their bark,
Bleed an accusing gum,
And in the unclean dark
The harpies come.

Integrity deceives
Itself in seeking a place;
My hand would bleed on the leaves,
The glass would shatter my face.

Blood on my hand and yours,
And all over the mind
A stone constriction, a force
Unhappy and unkind.

Where in the great hospitals
Or in the whimpering dark
Could Orpheus find madrigals
To bind the trees' bark?

Maynard's was such a time as ours,
Whip, dagger, and rack,
Tinder and flint for the poor house,
Black care at the back

Of every horseman, but he,
Though Europe is always a wound
Sought in his mind his integrity,
Sought, pondered, and found.

You and I are in his case,
No better and no worse.
In a fierce time a gentle face
And a consoling verse.

Three Profiles from Cairo

X

I thought chiefly of a
cat which approaches one,
rubs up against one's ankles,
then stalks away aloofly —
purr meaning spite and pleasure!
This elegant form curling
in its chair, and lapping up
its drink in a tidy fashion.

Some people's hairs bristle:
others (myself) like cats.

Y

As a child hides itself in a corner
(this face had a ruined beauty)
this face would hide behind the long
gesturing hands, or a new story,
or cold beer in a glass.

A face requiring lights and mirrors,
the painter, the photographer,
all the projections of Narcissus,
requiring evening and the wineglass:
dead face of the afternoons.

Thrust forward by an irrelevant
moving-on-its-own-path
river of war—and with the tide,
and near the shore: floating,
but with a sulky look as if to say,
'I choose, I *choose* to drift!'

I am reminded of a
lost child in the streets of Glasgow
whose hopes of home slowly founder
in that enormous labyrinth,
turning as the evening falls
to lighted windows in a sweetshop:
how bright the gaslight glitters,
how lucid are the colours,
how far the quiet bedroom
with all its blue pictures,
how far the green meadows,
how far the love!

Z

You, sir, whom everybody hates
because of your reptilian coldness
and the cold-cream unction
of your inedible voice,

whom we are tempted, too, to envy
since with a careful pumice
you smooth your dreary poems,
you, accomplished sir,

whom other poets fear
because your judgements are
cold, academical,
perception winged by spite,

talking in the serene evening
of food and drink in England,
I found you not unpleasant:
and thought with some amusement
of all those poems in which
lust points its knife against you...
and what a placid fellow
such a cruel poet is!

And had the sudden fancy:
this is no cold serpent,
coiling its cruel loves,
rather a kindly Indian
fluting his careful measure
(all its foul fangs extracted)
to his tame snake.

The End of a War

It's seven years ago to-day you told me
That seven years might see it at an end,
So, in the fairy tales, it's seven years
The seven brothers are transformed to swans.
It's seven years their sister sows with nettles
Their jerkins, seven years she must not speak,
They put their jerkins on, but one's unfinished:
The bright knight has the shoulder of a swan.

I see no parallel. Except it's seven
Years for us, backwards, if we wish to take
Up in our magical hands the undamaged city,
It is seven small bright years, like years in stories,
All small and bright with pain. They crackle
Under my verse like phosphorous on a spoon.
The battles and the speeches are like clockhands.

They are spiky crystals we hesitate to touch;
They stab and hurt so. Like a frozen wave,
A hollow shape, where now we cannot drown,
But still some selves of ours are drowning there:
Or like the death mask of a violent man,
That still can halt us with a mimic terror:
I fear to drown in the photograph of a wave.

Here from the shore, the shallows, I look back:
Not on an ocean, but a flat projection,
Fatal, unaltered, each arrested gesture:
Hoffman leaning on a stick at Brest-Litovsk,
With the falling snow in the photograph always
About to fall: and Hoffman leans on his stick,
The self-indulgent Prussian in glasses,
Under the unreal snow, in a glass ball.

We shake it for a snow-storm. History
Was once this trick the fancy played at firesides...
But a war is at an end, and that demands of me
Unusual eloquence; Sassoon had a feeling
After the last one, 'everyone suddenly burst out
Singing. And the singing never would end.'

But so many shapes are frozen into the snow
Of the grey snapshot; including shapes of myself!

The representation has quite swallowed the will.
We cannot put the will in the static picture.
The sadist becomes the *voyeur,* the revivalist
Compiles like Dante a Baedeker of Hell,
The great figures of history become Irvings:
Marionettes, we may choose to pull the strings
And Hitler will dance again; as Napoleon
Has danced in a hundred mad imaginations,

His hundred biographers. The farther they get
From willing it, like Bainville on Napoleon,
The smaller and the brighter grow the years,
Drained of the pain. They represent the truth,
The thing that we can handle and cannot alter.
They say, 'It was that way, it had to be,'
They never suffered from blitz or diarrhoea
Or waiting for the news. They never had it,

They lost no lovers in their neat sharp wars.
They never saw the moving wave of history,
They never swam in it; they never gripped at
The flat sand yielding to the nails, God's shore.
They never knew the truth of the illusion,
Or how the blind will makes illusion true...
But all I loved like seven swans have flown
For seven years, not knowing human speech.

And her ten fingers that I loved have sown
Me seven nettle jerkins. It is more true, that,
Than what to-day they'll tell us in the papers,
When the knights put on their jerkins, they did not sing,
The human tears rolled down their cheeks, their sister
Could speak at last in an inhuman voice,
A voice grown rusty; and the youngest brother,
He still had the bright shoulder of a swan.

It's how it happens, it's the pathos, it's
The apathy of pathos. My six bright swans are frozen
Into their six bright skies. The end is happy
But just in the manner of a fairy tale
That must have its stale extravagant sadness first.
My seventh swan could not survive the poem.
You listen through the sadness silently:
It's when the happy ending comes you cry.

Letter from Asmara, May, 1943

(For H.T.)

I write to you from the high air, from the shabby
Colonial town that laid Ethiopia dead,
Mountains romantic in Prokosch's geography
But not to a Sergeant with a Sunday morning head,

And if I had ever cared for the properties,
The evocative names that make poetry go with a swing,
Gura, Nefacit, Ambulagi, Keren,
I have had my fill this year—but I look at the thing,

At the 'dying Empire': Fascism sits unshaved
Drinking its morning bibita in the café,
Discussing the latest radiodiscorsa of Ansaldo
Or Colonel Stevens—but happy either way

That war at last is a matter of talk and maps,
With no horrible messages hurtling out of the sky:
No need to die for the bombastic phrases:
Men die less easily than Empires die,

And the smooth Inglesi, who win all wars, and talk
Of war with detachment or unaffected regret
Are pleasanter masters than the blond Tedeschi:
Though who is certain of the outcome yet?

I write from one of these strategic places
Where history, not love or verse, is made,
And where men sigh for Aberdeen or Parma
As endless pointless poker games are played,

The winnings to be spent on lime-and-whisky
(A new and barbarous colonial taste):
These evening sessions tend to be repeated:
These days repeat each other, with no haste.

It would be futile, in this air, like you
To sculpture verse or crystallise a myth;
A shabby myth himself the traveller;
Who once had lovers; who remembers kith,

Who notes how women in this climate dry,
But chatters bad French to a Syrian
Dropped in his sex like pebbles in a tarn
Making small circles: sex takes what it can.

His life, the legionary's, who holds together
The Empire that too tediously falls,
Uneasy, when he hears the Roman gossip,
His tastes no longer are the capital's:

But thinking wistfully of Alexandria,
Where he could swim and polish up his Greek,
Cadge lunches from the literary exiles,
Talk, in the wineshops (in the mess, you *speak*).

And thanking God, at least, the German border,
Always in trouble, is so far away:
That Caesar, here, is propped with little effort:
And that his pension will be due some day.

The soldier is a cosmopolitan,
You cannot trust his habits or his tastes:
He likes to hear the news from home in letters,
But readily returns towards his wastes.

From the short leave in London, longed-for meetings
That are somehow less rewarding than he expects
(That Time fades other beauties, too, distresses
Who other coldness than his own detects.)

For the moment is rare, and blurs, and the daily
Imperfect habit creates its needed routine.
Love grows too clamorous. And sense too savage.
Writing too difficult. And thought, too keen.

Drown all in liquorish good-fellowship!
Rarely at night you'll stir upon your bed
Agonised by the irresolvable distance
Of some too fair, too well-remembered head,

Rarely at night you'll clutch the pillow and cry...
This myth grows shy and chary of its tears.
I post it as a gift for your collection
Across enormous oceans of dumb years,

You, perhaps, can set it acting and moving,
A personage in your panorama of verse;
Smooth my rough lines, enrich my barren images,
While I new roles in harsher halls rehearse.

Three Characters in a Bar

(Cairo, 1944)

One who wishes to be my friend,
One who at sight hates my face,
Drinking late at the same bar.

Lurching colonial character
Technicoloured and wired for sound:
'Why don't you hurry out of this place?'

Charming gentle bohemian
Last, last of the Jacobites
Lighting my countless cigarettes:

'Pleasant to meet indeed, old man!
No one to talk to all these nights
About the prompters behind the sets.'

And there over behind the bar
A mirror showing my own face
That shows no love, that shows no hate

That cannot get out of its own place
And must hear me talking at night:
I drink to you, long-sufferer!

The Landscape

The world's a landscape that we see as whole
But must describe in detail. It's a world
Whose poetry is the unexpected detail,
But if the detail falls too far apart
The poet may forget there is a world;
But if the whole is grasped immediately
Nothing can prove our grasp of it was proper.

I thought of this theme once in Palestine,
A tired cadet, watching a sand-table,
A little landscape for my liquid eye:
Rivers of tape and matchbox houses, hills
Of sand concealing pigmy gun-emplacements,
And I'd to move imaginary soldiers
Over a cardboard bridge or perhaps over
A ford there might be, or might not, but where
There was less dead ground concealing enemies.

You think in abstracts then: height, distance, danger.
My trouble was I saw it as a landscape.

Our trouble is we see it as a landscape:
Nothing can prove our grasp of it is proper.
The poem must ignore height, distance, danger.
It holds the landscape in a liquid eye,
A landscape real, but that you'll never walk in,
And the sharp world says: 'Duck!' or 'Make your plans!'

Our plan is merely to regard the landscape
As if we had invented it (we have not)
And feel, not think, that pain, height, distance, danger;
And so we feel a power that comes to nothing
The moment we would put it to a use.

If all I balance is my own sensation
Or some identical shell of colour and shape
Peeled from the real and screened upon my nothing
When my sharp eye has scraped the picture off
Where is the real landscape I do not have?
Nowhere at all unless the poem screens it,
A balanced landscape in the liquid eye.
My poems are the colours of my nothings,
The claims of my evasions to apply.

A Winter Letter

(To my sister in London, from Asmara)

Like an unnourished rose I see you now, and yours the
Pallor of that city of soot and pigeons
Where the leaf is pale, that seems to curl its tendrils
Always around the painted green of iron,
I imagine you pale among the pigeon droppings,
And with your eyelids shadowed like the violets
They sell in bunches from their pavement baskets,
And I imagine you not with your old buxomness
But slim like the young ladies in the advertisements,
With your hair preened in a mode of cockney smartness
And your hands in the pockets of a heavy coat...
Do you think wistfully as I do, my darling,
These mornings when your heart is not in that city,
Reluctant stroller to the Board of Trade,
Of our glittering and resourceful north, with its
Terminus smell in the morning of cured herrings
And its crackling autumn suburbs of burned leaves?
Though I write in winter, and now except for the hollies
The trees in our old garden are all bare:

82

Now as they walk these streets of flashing mica,
They puff white steam from their nostrils, men and horses,
And their iron heels strike out sparks from the frosty road!
Now the white mist seeps round the red brick baths by the sea-front
And the children are girning at play with blue fingers
For a sea-coal fire and the starch of a Scotch high-tea,
Now with nipped red cheeks, the girls walk the streets rapidly,
And the shop-window's holly and tinsel can hardly delay.
I think of the swirl of the taffeta schoolgirls at Christmas,
Remembering Bunny whose skin was like cream upon milk,
Remembering Joy with her honey-dark skin and dark glances,
Remembering Rosemary's chatter and eloquent eyes,
Ahimé! and sigh because war with its swoop and its terror
That pounces on Europe and lifts up a life like a leaf,
Though its snell wind whirl you into a niche where you're cosy,
Yet its years eat up youth and the hope of fulfilment of youth.

And last night I dreamt I returned and therefore I write,
Last night my train had drawn up at a black London station,
And there you were waiting to welcome me, strange but the same,
And I shook your gloved hands, kissed your light-powdered cheek, and was
    waiting
To see your new flat, and your books, and your hats, and your friends,
When I suddenly woke with a lost lonesome head on my pillow,
And black Africa turning beneath me towards her own dawn,
And my heart was so sore that this dream should be snapped at the prologue
That I send you my soreness, dear heart, for the sake of this dream.

Three Sonnets for a Wedding

(From Asmara, for J. and F.)

I stand and think of you in broken corners;
The sun on barrels, heaps of lime, and staves.
What can I wish you, what gift can I bring
From this unwatered country, from this high
Rock city, where the liquid noontide laves
My stony corners: where the shadows lie
Like pools of grief upon a stony house?
Would your face warm, your hands tremble and sing
Among the heaps of lime and staves, because,
Although the broken house will have its mourners,
These speak of a new building, a time not shut
On love? Virginity's a brave house, but
It leaves no chink for the intrusive mouse
Whose little love can only creep through flaws.

I sit and think of you at beer-hall tables;
A woman plays on an accordion.

What can I wish you, what gift can I bring
From old Vienna? If I could recall
A tune whose melody goes on and on!
Hops, muslin, apples: girls who smell of all
These simple scents, and smell of soap and water:
A solid wooden shape for everything
These evenings with the crack of cabbies' whips,
The light of cafés, and the whiff of stables,
A world made one by music, where you know
Nothing that ever comes need ever go;
And every servant girl is beauty's daughter
And every soldier has your lover's lips.

I lie and think of you in army blankets:
The long night heavy with desire and grief.
What can I wish you, what gift can I bring
From vain desire? Perhaps its dreaming shape,
Love, like an autumn, falling leaf by leaf,
Grave of desire no lover can escape,
Venus above my couch, my grief defeated,
Whose firm and ghostly arms about me cling—
Now happy in his more solid arms you lie!
Love has so many disillusions: thank its
Illusions for a little time at least.
It is a warm, companionable beast
And a most loyal angel, well entreated,
Who'll not desert you, darling, till you die.

s.s. City of Benares

(Drowned refugee children, 1940)

The bell that tolls my syllables can tell
An underwater tale, clang how there fell
Suddenly out of a surface shouting world
Into dumb calm doomed children, and there curled
(Currents' sick fingers whispering at their hair)
Round them a coiling clutch, was our despair.
Sea's soft sad pressure, like the sprawl of love,
Darkly spreadeagled, so they could not move,
The wide wet mouth was heavy, they would choke,
Till in that cold confusion pity spoke:
'This is a nightmare and one is asleep.
This is a dream, my brave one, do not weep,
Often may drown in dreams and not be dead:
Such weight is mother leaning on your bed.'

But having thought of this to cheat my pain,
That woe and wonder harrows me again,

Fat clouds seem bulked like whales, while through the green
Grave tons of twilight, in a submarine
Solidity of air like sea I move,
Pressure of horror how our hate hurts love.
Deeper than grief can plummet, mercy lies,
But not so deep as trust in children's eyes,
Justice is high in heaven, but more high
Blood of the innocent shall smear the sky—
Or think that red the flame of seraph wings,
See stained-glass heaven, where each darling sings
In God's dark luminous world of green and gold
As lovely as death's waters, but less cold:
Think what you will, but like the crisping leaf
In whipped October, crack your thoughts to grief.
In the drenched valley, whimpering and cold,
The small ghosts flicker, whisper, unconsoled.

On Roosevelt's Death

All the weak good, and all the wicked great,
He knew them all. He was the good great man,
Jut jaw, grey parchment grin! It seemed too late,
So many voices babbling, so much hate,
Envy, and policy, but he could span,
Grave, patient, eloquent, the gulf that ran
Between their dream of hometown and their fate.
The weak and good who wanted whisky still,
And fun, and wanted it to be like peace,
Listened to goodness in authority:
The wicked great saw his good strength increase,
The lion's strength, the fox's policy:
And the unwilling found in him their will.

To Chloe

(From D'Annunzio's version of the Latin of Horace)

Chloe, you avoid me like a young fawn
Through mountain thickets seeking for its anxious
    Mother, not without foolish
    Fears of leaves and breezes,

So if the thorn-bush shivers in the breezes
Its fidgety leaves, or if the virid
    Lizard should streak across the path,
    Heart and knees tremble...

But I like a horrid tiger or a greedy
Lion do not follow you to gulp you...!
      For you are old enough to wed,
      Chloe, and leave mama.

To Furius and Aurelius

(From D'Annunzio's version of the Latin of Catullus)

Furius and Aurelius, to me sweet companions,
Whether from the extreme Indies I go to the rock
Which the world's-edge long-resonant wave
      Whips at for ever:

Or among the Hyrcanians and lecherous Arabs
Or Persians I move or arrow-shooting Parthians
Or where the Nile from her seven mouths
      The sea colours:

Or whether I cross the high Alps snowy,
Of our great Caesar the monuments admiring,
Or reach the yellow Rhine or of Britain
      The unpolished people,

You, whom, with me, to distrust each event
The Gods instruct, make your souls ready,
These brief—bear back to my love—
      Bitter sayings:

'Live and enjoy yourself with your thirty gallants,
Helping them to spend their disgusting riches,
Loving none of them, and of all in equal measure
      Breaking the haunches;

'Live and despise my love that falls
Through a fault of yours just as a flower
On the edge of a field that the hard plough
      Touches in passing.'

To Neaera

(From D'Annunzio's version of the Latin of Horace)

It was night with the shine of the moon 'mid the smaller stars shining,
    And no night could be clearer,
When you (but you schemed then already to cheat the Immortals)
    You swore to me, traitress,

And tighter around me your sensuous arms were clinging
　　　　Than ivy to ilex,
'While the wolf to the flock—or, as deadly to steersmen, Orion
　　　　Excites winter storms,

'While in dawnlight still shiver the long golden locks of Apollo,
　　　　This love shall be ours!'
But take care lest the day should arrive when my firmness, Neaera,
　　　　Shall bring you misfortune,

Because if poor Flaccus has still in these veins but one drop
　　　　Of manly blood throbbing,
He'll not suffer the strenuous nights it's your pleasure to grant
　　　　To a lustier rival,

But will seek in his anger another girl to requite him
　　　　With an equaller love,
You are lovely, but loyalty pardons you only the first time
　　　　When the torture is real.

And you, sir, whoever you are, lucky dog, sir! Walk sprucely:
　　　　Make mock of my fall:
Have fat flocks and great holdings: and over the limestone rock flow
　　　　Your sun-dappled streams,

Let Pythagoras fail to surpass you in modish abstruseness,
　　　　Nireus in looks...
Aye me! you'll weep too for the lover to another conceded:
　　　　My turn to laugh!

Rhétorique Sentimentale du Temps d'Hiver

Ornée de feuilles, d'eaux vives et de cygnes
et de chacun de tes arbres dans le bronze éternel,
tu es, ma vallée, toute enclose des routes de métal!
Sous la tristesse des cyprès, le pauvre n'aura point de pique-niques,
ni les amoureux ne dormiront sur la mollesse des gazons...
En ce lieu, le dimanche, auprès des eaux,
quand fuient les nuages muets sur l'immensité des champs,
je m'assierai, triste, et regarderai les sombres voiles flottants.

Madame, vous savez l'histoire et le temps qui fut
sous les sycomores. Vous avez écouté le chant d'amour
à l'endroit où les saules tremblent sur le courant.
Cette saison, mais il faut nous hâter,
cette saison jamais ne reviendra:
j'en ai perdu tous les jours au fil de mon rêve.

Grande et noble, que vos fortes mains retiennent
les graines ailées pour l'automne. Hélas, ils ne sont que pour moi
tous printemps stériles et les stériles hivers,
mais les pesantes fleurs et les fruits les plus mûrs
sont pour vous seule dans tout leur suc et chargés de sève lourde...
Jamais, mon aimée, o tête si fière et profil pur,
ne seriez touchée d'aucun hiver
ni scellés les mots de vos lèvres ni votre sourire, o
tendresse oubliée qui me fut une fois et présente
et dispensée quoiqu'obscure avec mystère,
quelle mort vous prendrait, quelle vieillesse!

Ni jamais ne seriez moins aimable
si je connaissais les mots qui suspendent la saison!
Hélas, votre monde facile, hélas, votre sourire, s'attendent
à la perte soudaine: moins permanent que ce paysage
est le destin avec lenteur d'une argile vivante:
la chair porte la mort.
Et vous m'oublierez, la victime d'un mot et d'un sourire.

Ou si serai cruel et solitaire
et tel moi-même l'imprenable forteresse,
plus dur mon désespoir coulé dans le roc sur la tendre vallée,
je me dresserai, ultime promontoire sur tout le paysage dominé,
et symbole triste par le vent d'indifférence frappé
ainsi que la grimace immobile des gargouilles dans la tempête,
ou le fou errant, insensible sous les pluies...

Mais, o pitié sur moi, si serai pitoyable
autant que la rose égarée dans l'hiver,
ou tout discours au moment des adieux
si ce monde du regard, ce monde cruel
contre l'épaisse lame séparatrice de l'œil
est celui qui se dérobe à l'impuissante main
O monde qui n'existes seulement que pour nos déchirements
et seulement, mes larmes, que pour nos défaites!

Ah! Ne vous laissez tromper par douces paroles
ni ne croyez surtout aux faciles pardons...
Chère, n'osez m'imaginer ni tranquille auprès du feu, ni
installé en la securité, celui que les musiques distraient:
sachez que le jour lève sur l'abîme du cœur
contre vous, mon amour, je me tiendrai du côté des vaincus,
tel le héros tragique et, triste, écoutant l'appel,
malgrè les grands pensers qui furent, à jamais l'unique
des jeunes années du temps d'amour. O jour
ainsi qu'un grand orage, ainsi que la nue noire,
du sort lourdement suspendu, à jamais retenu,
oh! sans relâche ni détente d'aucune pluie à jamais,
et qui plonge à travers toute obscurité, cadavre, mon âme,
aux ailes toutes grandes de givre insultées,
avide et seul, l'oiseau archaïque, le cormoran!

O plus pitoyable que la mort des pauvres,
ou comme le visage aveugle plus pâle dans la peur,
est mourant à soi-même l'amour dans la solitude,
parce que les mains pour les caresses furent malvenues,
parce que les mots se turent qui ne furent pas répondus,
et qu'une seule voie s'ouvre loin du ridicule qui stigmatise:
O fierté des vaincus, sacrifice dans la haine et la douleur,
et l'élégance de Domitien mourant au salon des glaces,
et l'ultime glaive!
      Va, mon cœur, vis
avec la seule mort; l'orgueil du coursier t'emporte
aux défaites, fiancé condamné des tendresses perdues!

A Legend of Franz Josef

Imagine an old man's abstract head
In a landscape growing dull and dead.
A long training in looking noble
Has seen him through the years of trouble.
But now he has grown slack and sick
With a slower pulse than a clock's tick
And his pattering footsteps seem to mock
The clock's mournful *tock tock*
Or shuffling on the parquet floor
In carpet slippers, he seems no more
A tired old man whom time bereaves
But a gardener's rake among the leaves.
And in his palaces now neurosis
Fragile as the rococo poses
Of Maria Theresa's peacocks, screams.
Nobody dreams that the old man dreams
But his snow roofs lie huddled under
A mad spire. Blunder on blunder
Has led His Patriots to expose
His Austrian Archduchy to snows
That lie, a candy winding-sheet,
On palaces you'd love to eat,
With marble grapes, and enamel birds,
And stucco icing, the cream and curds
Of clouds and cherubs, the acid plop
Of a chandelier that seems to drop
Small crystal sweetmeats to the lips
Or lemonade in dew-drop sips.
Poor old man! and when he was younger
He felt the stony Habsburg hunger,
But the stone lion that stands beneath
The shield is dying with broken teeth...
Habsburgs saved Europe from the Turk
But the poor old man is past his work
And the gruel that he sips for his evening posset
Has a bony taste of the skeleton closet

And his hard and narrow iron bed
Torments his stolid soldier's head.
His son is dead and unforgiven,
Shamed upon earth, and barred from heaven,
A suicide and a murderer:
(But his anger fires when he thinks of her,
'Madame, your unfortunate daughter...',
O ice for her, and fire, and water,
And if damned to hell his son must be,
O let her share his eternity!)

And long ago a murderer's knife
Had killed his dear cantankerous wife.
(And little peace with her he's had;
But all the Wittelsbachs were mad.)

'Tyrol, Carinthia, Tuscany...'
He mouths them over; but let them be,
He cannot warm his old cold hands
At any hunger of Habsburg lands.
All he sees are enormous snows
And how little and cold he grows,
And he wonders...but can it be
Bad times have come for The Family?

'The magic mirror's near at hand
That Kepler gave to Ferdinand
And if one will brave the luck—and mine
Is not so happy I need repine—
The magic mirror will show the face
Of the next to stand in the Archduke's place
At the table head on the Hofburg floor
As Arch-Duke and as Emperor
Come ten, come twenty, come thirty year—
Just as the question makes it clear.'

He whispered, 'If this shows bloody work
So did the sack of Magdeburg;
If it does no honour to me or mine,
Nor did the killing of Wallenstein;
If it tatters the sky with blood and tears
So did the war of Thirty Years.'

And the word was the War of Thirty Years:
He pulled the curtain and watched his fears,
But all that he saw in the mirror was
A Why reflecting a great Because,
Or a vacant No suggesting Yes:
A glass drank up an emptiness...

The mirror clouded with his breath
Which meant the next day brought his death.

'Well,' he said, 'we have done our work.
We saved the Empire from the Turk.
(Or if Jan Sobieski did,
He was Our servant, when all's said,
And by the Donau's bloody banks
Rode Leopold to give him thanks.)
We built. And we were kind to art.
(But note down Schubert and Mozart.)
We fought. We married. We had lands.
The case is written and it stands...'

The mirror pearled to silver frost
Which meant the luck of the line was lost.

'Metternich,' he chuckled, 'how
Would you plan your Europe now?
With all your papers scattered, for
You used a room as a *coffre-fort*
And when at night you locked the door
Europe lay scattered on the floor!
But you are dead. You have no key
To lock together My lands for Me,
And the wind will blow them from this great room
To that interminable gloom —
Venetia, Trieste, Budapest:
Like papers fluttering from a desk!'

The mirror turned black, which meant
It was the moment to repent.

'God,' he said, 'I am old and tired.
I have not had what I desired.
Have grown stiff, past loves and hates,
With stewarding of My Estates,
Have grown a tired old man of wood,
A creaking puppet, kind and good
To country children, and a giant
Brutal and bloody to defiant
Small angry nationalities:
At last they bring me to my knees
And like a mangy dog, beneath
The shield I die with broken teeth...
But I am tired. I am glad to die.
To see Earth changing and not know why,
To lay at last my sick old head,
With an easy heart, on my soldier's bed.
God, for my sins, forgive me, if
My own forgiveness, grown so stiff,
Still turns this creaking heart of wood.
O fading glass, have I been good?
I held the world decaying in my hand.
Why it decays I do not understand.'

That night the storm shocked the people
And rocked and shook St Stephen's steeple
And when the morning came, like thunder
The great bells clanged on high, and under
The spire the little houses clung.
While loud and sad and iron rung
The knell of the old Emperor.
Whose soul has fled. We pray therefor.

Prelude

(From Gabriel D'Annunzio)

Goes the brown cameleer by the tawny deserts of Arabia:
Tediously stretch the tawny sands, undulating around.

The sun like an archer shoots cursed flames at his temples,
Burns the blood in his pulses, yellows his eyes with gall.

There sprout by the way heads, unburied and horrible;
Shamelessly naked the thigh-bones; naked curve the ribs.

Heads of black slaves these, dead in ferocious agony:
Against the mute solitude imprecating in vain.

They look, they look, with their empty eyes a long way,
They look for the palms with their benign shade.

O brown cameleer—and like to the heads here sprouting—
No need to bestir yourself; such is your destiny too.

Plods the brown cameleer, plods, plods; one need in his aching,
Felt in the heart of him for an antique sweetness...

O Namuna, Namuna, the shining daughter of Nagda,
With the eyes of a water-buck, the river-flow of your hair...

O sweet were our colloquies 'neath the high palm-trees of Gada,
In the plenilunar whiteness, in the rich sunsets of gold.

Plod, plod; the camel, used up, slackens its paces:
The sun over the head of us and the sand and the sand before.

O Allah is great!... To the withering eye there is smiling,
Near at hand an oasis, grateful in all its green!

There the palms appear upwards, proud in frondage and fruitage,
And a thousand blossoms brilliantly interlace.

There birds are mingling chants joyous and amorous,
And water running freshly has a suave sound.

There the noble water-buck pastures in the shadow
And humming throngs of insects prismatically shine,

And to eyes ravaged by sunlight the soft greens are restful:
And a placid freshness flows in the rested veins.

Rides the brown cameleer alert now: and less long the journey
To his senses, less hard the way, less fiery the sun.

Such, O divine Muse, when your great eyes turn benignly,
Such a joyous rainbow shines anew in my heart:

Then my lucid phantasms laugh as in festival,
Through skies of cobalt and through enchanted seas;

Then I lose slowly in the breeze the golden cumuli,
Slowly then the white sails, they slowly shift away...

And all hail, O my goddess! Glut others with verse that rumbles
Round in its wooden stanzas, the chariot greased with rhyme.

To me concede the short strophe, that strains and needs checking,
And finally trembles, a tamed steed, under my strong hand.

The Melancholy of a Fine Day

(From Pierre Jean Jouve)

Trees are enormous in the rainy summer.
One doesn't know the sky there's so much moonshine,
Silver, with a radiant redness under the clouds,
No sun. Or look at it from the wrong end,
You see a single day implacably fine and warm,
An implacable unrolling and display of a fine day,
And the howling and beaten earth makes a shadow
And the birds are flying with slouched, flattened wings,
And space with its hands of azure clutches itself,
Its breast groans under its azure hands.

While the town is encumbered with accustomed heats
And the girls dry their slick hair or their stupor
In the bosom of a fine day.

O God! let these pretty girls be preparing to die
And let summer be such an obscure season in this quarter
That six million inhabitants may pass by here
Without really remaining more than an hour,

O God, there are far too many inanimate worlds,
On the contrary, there's not enough imminent death:
That statue
That stirs heavily shifting its raised breasts.

*Four Sonnets
from Guido Cavalcanti*

I

My foolish eyes, that first did look upon,
Lady, your all too formidable face,
Were those that did accuse me of you, on
A day when Love held court in his high place;
And laid their evidence before him there
That by his judgement I should be your slave —
What sighs and griefs did down upon me bear
And what a rashness in my heart did rave!
Then led me forth again, all pleas denied,
Into a place where seemed it there was none
But for Love's burden drew a sighing breath:
Who, when they saw me, all with pity cried,
'Now you are made the slave of such a one
That other hope you cannot have than Death!

II

You have in you the flowers and the green grass:
And what is shining or is fair to see:
Light of the sun your own light doth surpass:
Who hath not seen you, worthless wight must be!
And in this world of ours, no creature is
So full of pleasure and delightfulness:
If any man fear love, new courage his,
Seeing your face, so much himself to bless!
The ladies all, that bear you company,
For your dear sake, are pleasing to my sight,
And I would beg them of their courtesy,
To do you honour, each to strive her best,
And in your sovereignty to have delight
Since of them all you are the loveliest.

III

Who's this that comes, as each man looks at her,
Makes tremulous with clarity the air,
And leads Love with her, so that speak or stir
Can none among us: all have sighs to spare!
Alas? How seems she when her eyes she turns?
Let Love relate what I may not explain:
Yet such esteem her modest bearing earns
Another in her place shall earn disdain.

Uncounted are the gifts that make her rich:
To her the Gentle Virtues are obeisant:
Beauty, as Beauty's Goddess, doth approve her.
Nor was our mind tuned to so high a pitch,
Nor of its health so properly complaisant,
That we could have a proper knowledge of her.

IV

Beauty of ladies of compassionate heart
And cavaliers, in arms, and high in pride,
And singing birds, and lovers' rhetoric art,
And painted ships which on the strong seas ride,
And air serene at the first peep of dawn,
And blanchèd snow descending with no wind,
And watery bank, and flower-adornèd lawn,
And ornaments with azure and gold refined,
So much her beauty and her nobleness
Surpass, and such a courage do they carry,
Those seem but stale in the beholder's eye:
So much more knowledge in her looks doth lie
As the low earth than the high heaven is less:
To such a one good luck will never tarry.

Perch'i' no Spero...

(From Guido Cavalcanti)

Since I do not hope to return ever,
Little ballad, to Tuscany,
Go thou, swift and sleight,
Unto my lady straight
Who, of her courtesy,
Will give thee gentle cheer.
Thou shalt bring news of sighs,
Of deep grief, of much fear:
But guard that none thy journey spies
Who's enemy to gentleness:
Or, sure, for my unhappiness,
Thou'lt be delayed
And so assayed
'Twill be my pain,
Past death, to plain
New grief and many a tear.
Thou feel'st how death, O little song,
Clippeth me close in whom life endeth:
Thou feel'st this heart to beat too strong
So fierce each vital sprite contendeth.
So much consumèd is this body now
Its suffering is done, I trow:

Thou, for thy part,
Thou then, prithee,
Take thou this soul with thee
Whenever forth it issueth from my heart.
'Las! little ballad! for thy amity
This trembling soul I recommend thee:
Bear it with thee, with all its pity,
To that sweet fair to whom I send thee.
'Las! little ballad! say with a sigh
When thou stand'st her before:
'Here doth your servant lie
Come to make stay with you
Parted from him who
Was Love's servitor.'
And thou, bewildered and enfeeblèd voice,
Now from this sore heart weeping issue find,
And with this soul and with this little song
Go reasoning of this exhausted mind.
There thou wilt find a lady pleasurable
And of a mind so choice
'Twere thy delight if able
To go her ways before,
My soul: and her adore
For her true worth, for ever.

In un Boschetto

(From Guido Cavalcanti)

There in a woodland, to my thought more bright
Than a star's light, I found a shepherdess.
Her hair she had golden and ringleted,
And her eyes full of love, rosy her hue:
With a small switch her lambs she pasturèd,
And being barefoot, she was bathed with dew.
Singing she was, as though with love she burned,
And was adorned with all delightfulness.
With love I did salute her thereupon
And asked if she had any company
Whereto she answered in a gentle tone
Alone, alone she walked that woodland way,
And said: 'Know thou, that when the birds complain
Then I am fain, a lover to possess.'
No sooner had she told me her condition
And through the wood I heard the birds to sing
Than in myself I said: 'Now is the season
Out of this shepherdess my joy to wring.'
Mercy I asked her that to kiss with lips
And love with clips, she should have willingness.

And then my hand she took most amorously
And said her heart a gift to me she made
And led me underneath a shadowy tree
Where many a flower I saw of every shade
And such a joy and sweetness to me brought,
I saw, methought, the god of tenderness.

The Begetting of a Poet

(From the French of Stéphane Mallarmé)

Because the roast was served up piping hot,
Because the newspaper described a rape,
Because, about her base, ill-buttressed throat,
The slut forgot to fasten up her cape,

Because from the bed, huge as a sacristy,
He saw upon the clock a satyrs' rout,
Or because he could not sleep, and with no modesty
Under the sheets, his leg sought her leg out,

The oaf, on top, his cold dry dame beneath,
To her white bonnet put his tasseled cap,
And worked away, grunting tremendously:

No night of comets, nor no thunderclap,
But two dull creatures coupling sleepily,
Shakespeare or Dante, drew you from the sheath!

Poem from a Spanish Model

Childhood, green meadow, bell tower, palm,
Mosaic window Sun, wandering butterfly,
Hanging upon the vernal afternoon
In the azure zenith, like a rosy kiss:

Sealed garden! In you a single bird is singing
Through all the green tinged with melodious gold:
Soft and fresh wind! You also waft to me
The music of the bull-ring far away.

Ah, before the unspeakable sourness of the fall
That wrapped in rusty crêpe my grieving heart,
Young nightingale, I loved on satin evenings
The complete silence or the fountain's noise.

Paul Valéry

Who knows, what lasts, what crumbles? He,
While all the rest were talking, sat apart,
Indifferent to the noise of history
And the untutored message of the heart,

Indifferent to the pattern of the stars,
Kant was too simple there, and Pascal blind,
Their rhetoric was vague; but certain bars
Of music gave their measure to his mind,

And made him follow with a formal care
Some boyish problem of identity
Most of us thought of once. It led us where
We found it puzzling, so we let it be,

Why I am *I,* and yet another Me
Plays its escaping tricks? What I observe
Is never Me observing—can I see
What casts my shadows, while my shadows swerve?

One life was not too long to ponder that.
Perhaps there were no solids there at all
But shadows of a shadow on the flat
Expanse of nothing that was not a wall.

Stare long enough, the world itself can seem
Like some word children will go on and on
Repeating—'Oh, a dream, a dream, a dream!'
Is that word found in any lexicon?

Is it a word we have made up ourselves?
Perhaps we have made up the self with words,
There are too many books on all our shelves:
O self, my multiple conceptual birds!

Narcissus needed mirrors to be real
But choked in merging with reality,
The mind, a single nowhere, swoons to feel
Its multilocal multiplicity.

And, if we dream, the mind is not a glass,
But, like the sea, a blind and brutal thing,
Opaque and surly, clangorous as brass:
Waking's a standing pond in which we fling

Pebbles of thought to watch the ripples spread,
To watch the ripples vanishing away!
The night reminded him he would be dead
After the scrutability of day.

Sleeping reminded him that life begins
A sleepy thing, sweet with confused desires,
Mild teasing impulses that prick like pins;
He kindled to be kindled in these fires.

Life was a fruit, and meant to be consumed,
But how its sweetness melted in the mouth!
The formal image of a woman loomed
Through all the argument, to slake his drouth,

But only for a moment, let her sleep
And let him watch her there, and contemplate
Her as the primal Eve. And let her weep,
For she must wake, and he her world create,

He, the cold serpent of the intellect,
The stinging bee beside the pulpy fruit.
O let there be no mirrors to reflect
Reflection at the Tree of Wisdom's root!

Like skiffs, his poems peck upon that sea,
The great, opaque, the brassy sea, the blind:
And in my mouth melts his mortality.
The thoughtless clay has drunk the thinking kind.

Summer and Winter

I

Summer can ripen common flesh on sea-shores
And makes its whorlings whisper like sea-shells:
Summer grows roses from the mouths of whores
And rings the changes on the seaside belles.
Summer, the dank, exhausted, and too pliant,
Can wash her sins away within the sea:
Summer the stones and grasses find compliant,
The waters flatter her ductility.
Summer, at evening, on her basket chair,
A blowsy frump, her glass of beer before her,
Can change her frock, put scent upon her hair,
And in the cool night we again adore her.
Be to her frailties a little blind:
Summer's a harlot but her heart is kind.

II

Winter has a diminishing sky:
And a perspective other than retrospect
That hurts and holds the eye.
Winter does not offer escape
Forward or backward from its final landscape
And on all sides its skies fall
As if the whole world were a theatre
Where the round year had taken its curtain call.
Winter offers us, for instance,
The nerves of a leaf on a puddle of ice
And the terrible nearness of distance.
As if, being aware, one stood
At the wrong, the small end of a corridor.
And winter has no analogy to war
Except the view of it the dying may have,
But is not unlike an unhappy love:
I love, but I do not like winter at all.

Song for Music

The fountains and the garden,
The garden and the ghost,
I lay my love before you
And do not count the cost
And know my love is lost.

I lay my love before you
For your unlucky hands
To break and spoil, but suffer
To suffer, while it stands,
What no one understands.

You will not break nor spoil it
Since you have other loves
Gathered with beaks as eager
Out of the air as doves
To peck your olive groves.

But suffer it to hover,
But suffer it to live,
Around the pools and fountains
Ghostly, where ghost birds dive
And both are fugitive.

Birds of the air, I call you,
Birds of the air, my throng,
Towards a ghost oasis
Where I shall linger long
But longer shall my song.

When images have faded
Like this delightful tree
Of mirage, like these waters
That were not meant to be,
My song, come back to me.

Come in another country
And with another coat
To smart my eyes to sobbing
And catch me by the throat
With these things of no note.

Ballad from Gongora

Weeping then the lady
And for this had reason
In the lengthened absence
Of ungrateful love,

Who had left her early:
And I hardly thought then
She had lived so long here
That he'd had time to go.

Weeping for the absence
Of the gallant traitor
Leaves her in the moonlight
And removes the sun.

She was adding always
Passion unto passion,
Memory to memory,
Piling grief on grief.

Therefore, heart, be weeping:
And for this have reason!

To the child the mother:
'Daughter, for my love now,
Overcome this weeping.
I am overcome.'

Whereto she responded:
'No, it cannot be, no.
Many are the causes
And the eyes are twain.

'Mother, let them act now
As bereft of reason
And the tears be falling
For a luckless chance.

'Wounds to make so many
In a single season
Shot he amorous arrows,
The little archer god!

'Now I sing not, mother,
And though I were singing
Many sorry stanzas
All my songs should be.

'He that has departed
With his other luggage,
Leaving me to silence,
Took away a voice.'

Therefore, heart, be weeping:
And for this have reason!

Musical Variations on the Death of Shelley

Death in a shell is music
And in a rose is odour
More urgent than earth's daughters
As more distilled and colder.
The killing rains come down:
The hope of change is gone,
I shall renounce the magic
Of inconsistent waters
A Christ can travel on.

Drown in the sea-king's daughters:
Death in a shell is rumour
And in a rose is odour
And inconsistent waters
I used to travel on,
And so the end is music
Like his who walked by magic
Upon the sea at Galilee
Where all the sailors drown.
Seas, open and devour me,
Before the seasons flower me
With roses; fiddle, crack, crack
(Spoil the road and I cannot come back)
Before the tune is done...
For if the tune should finish
And then the ear replenish

And then the ear grew coy,
Better to crack your fiddle,
And end it in the middle,
And still to keep your toy.

Like silks now tumble down
My sensualities,
The green lace dress, the powder
Brown on the ochre skin,
Like frothy waves of summer
(Though in the echo louder,
Though in my shell the louder)
They wander out and in.
But that was on the shore.
Death wears these silks no more.
And God and Plato frowning,
There's nothing left but drowning
In my consistencies.
The cavern teased with anger,
I shall not tease it longer,
It convolutes to flood.
Flushes.
　　　　The twirling plummet
Too often had gone down,
'The siege of pleasure lost,
Fractured the keel and only
The hope to be tossed battered —
The shrilling fret to finish —
Upon a pious coast.'

To sink or to go soaring
Beyond my shore-bound seas,
The surface minds of women,
Their sensualities:
My pale mask of the lover
And the philosopher
In callous, cold exploring
To trouble life no more:
Only a half-pay Captain
Drinking too much Marsala
To say, 'Yes, I knew Shelley!'
And see the talk lie fallow
And blush and twirl his glass:
'A fascinating fellow
But reputations pass!'

I never thought it mattered
If one could still replenish...
But if the Universal
In agonised dispersal
Were better gorged with blood?

And the Particular places
And hands and lips and faces
Were better? Plato frowning
(O sensualities!)
There's nothing left but drowning:
The cavern is in flood.

A Poet and his Ancestors

But love is the death
That my heart dies from...
John Waller

Spending the afternoon with Waller's loves,
Which he calls poems, I took pleasure in
Tracing ancestral echoes of a smooth
Plausible ghost, the elegant and thin

Clear lute of Edmund; Edmund's lovely rose
In John's pale garden lit a twilight air...
Edmund was tricky and political,
And so is John. That's neither here nor there,

For who remembers Waller's Plot? Or who
The General, that other ancestor,
'Waller the Conqueror,' who always lost
His larger battles in the Civil War?

And love was war for them, a garden war:
Whatever rose we pluck, the thorn has pricks.
So, too, in Edmund's time, they died from love
Between their battles and their politics.

And one recalls the ancient trimming rogue —
'The soul's dark cottage, battered and decayed' —
Having his joke with the sardonic Charles:
'Not truth, but fiction, is the poet's trade.'

'Waller was smooth: but Dryden taught to join' —
How does Pope say? — 'the long resounding line.'
And in a rough age smoothness pleases more
With flies in amber, and with sops in wine,

With girls, with roses. With a fiction. Now,
Reading John's lines with an oppressive heart
And knowing in them all the truth of fact,
I cannot judge them for the truth of art,

And think that Edmund with his Sacharissa
Perhaps was more sincere than we allow.
To know the poet and the person too
Is stupefying to the critic now.

'Tell her that wastes her time and me,' alas!
Or tell a Time that wastes itself and us
How all the real and daily deaths we die
Are mortal, but they are not amorous!

For the Marriage of Helen Scott and John Irwin

Call that man fortunate indeed
Who in such a time of winter
When our passions freeze and melt
And the city treads them under

Finds indeed, O crystal beauty,
Creature dauntless as the diamond,
That though love is sudden-stinging
Like the snowflake, it is mutual

Heat and pressure that engender
This sweet pain and many-pointed
Pleasure, enviable harshness,
Every facet flashing fire.

Call us fortunate who also
In one person's pleasing gestures,
Brittle seeming, frangible
In show, but in reality

(Since the Nefertiti profile
Seems of stone, and since the spirit
Is, like steel, resilient)
Strong in formal elegance,

Found a happiness in line and
Gesture that the muddy currents
Would and will not wash away:
Call her fortunate who is so.

Call occasion apt and congruous
That has brought her dream of crystal
To enclose his waking hours;
Call their contemplations active;

Call this augury a challenge
For one whose dream is real already
To make another's dreaming actual:
Call this marriage fortunate.

On a Memory of Beauty

How can the heart for sea and stone
    Be cumbered, and forget a face
That moved it once to fret and moan—
    Forget the woman, see the place?

But was it one or was it two,
    Was it a statue or a girl?
Might every spring her form renew,
    And the white sea-froth be her curl?

Beauty but for a moment shone,
    The likeness of a cloud or wave
Whose momentary aspect, gone,
    The sieve of memory cannot save.

Right at the back of my head I know
    Incredible wild things
Struggle like swans half-blind with snow—
    And the dying swan sings.

The Virgin, Bright and Beautiful To-day

(From Stéphane Mallarmé)

The virgin, bright, and beautiful to-day
Dare it now shatter with a drunken wing
This hard, forgotten lake, this ice where cling
These flights of mine that never flew away...
Once was a swan, remembers it is he,
Magnificent but hopeless in his strife,
For never having sung the realms of life
When winter shone in bleak sterility.
His neck in a white agony is shaken,
Shattering the space that mocks him for his pride
But not the soil in which his plumes are taken.
Phantom mere brightness to this scene has drawn,
Immobile in the cold, where dreams deride,
Clothed in the useless exile of the swan.

106

Summer Meditation

Luxurious the vacant heart,
That takes the steamy river in,
The feather-duster smell of trees,
The prickling promise of the day.

With the fine-teethed combs of thought
I hunt for malice in past sins
To shred and crumble malice out,

Easy, these mornings damp and fine,
To crack that louse upon my thumb,
To say, 'It was, and is not, mine.'

The dreary dandruff of the past
Lost in the summer's fine shampoo:
But will this washing be the last?

Our bodies are so like our souls,
Know staleness, acid, and decay,
But know recuperation, too,
And know the tempter on the way,

And know the little prickling pins
And know the alcoholic drum
From which a rhythmic message rolls:
'Days of excess were meant for you!'

Then, no new plot for summer's play?
And must I have the vacant part,
Follow the steam remote and thin
And smell the pepper-pot of ease,

Until I pause, and wake, and sneeze,
And all my promise drifts away,
Gone, like my coaxing, carnal heart,
That summer winkles with her pin?

Other Poems of the 1940s

You by the Unfamiliar River Walking

(For Tom Scott)

You by the unfamiliar river walking,
On the high bank over the pale green sky of your dream,
Where the faithless lovers return, and the new faces
Offer their unavailing solace, and your face meets with your face,
The drowned Narcissus, with the red mane streaming,
Streaming with a wake of bubbles, and a woman laughing,
The lost one lovely, on the high bank walking,
The whole air bubbling with drowning laughter;
And rigid and jointed the glittering meccano tower
Raises itself like a phallus on the scruffy plain,
And from the height you know the fear of falling:
Or propped like a toppling pillar, among the ferns
('Her name was Fearn, which suggested the scene!')
By the unasked-for love of a last night's acquaintance,
You caress her chastely with a natural gesture,
Her hand on your heart and yours on her silken thigh,
Consoling her as she sighs (the words in the dream
Become for once even the waking poem),
'Oh, that I might flow forever on your restful juices!'
You become aware, later in the dream, half-waking,
Of the railway station at midnight, iron and glass,
Disquieting noise of whistles, voices, hands,
Papers and chocolates — 'Oh remember, write!' —
Hell-shriek of siren and the tunnel gulps:
The poem is digested in the dark.

      And waking you are aware
Of the latent content of all these manifest beauties,
Of all these terrors; the uncertain border
Between the unreal sufferings of the real,
The soldiers hungry for food and words and love,
Gobbling at scraps like half-starved rats, and the real
Pathos and nobility of your personal fantasy:

You in a trivial suicide's world
Loyal to the long way round the majestic circuit
Of the human year, its summit of love and strife,
And the peace and death of its recurrent winter.

Oh you, at least, may you have a long summer.
Oh, let the way to your death at least be long.
Choose the circuitous way, and not like me
The green plants grown too white in their grey cellar,
And be for me, when my frail fingers snap
At last, the last of many fraying threads,
A true memorial, a juster image,
On my white screen a huge projected shadow,
The tall, the lonely, and the too much loved;
So from my grave may green fulfilment grow,
My ghost find peace in its authentic hero.

The Time

The time demands a rolling eye,
Demands an indecisive gesture,
Demands a slithering journalist's look
Pinned to no point, but quick for all,
Demands the most extended concept
Of pain, or politics, or cities
And screams against intensities,
Calls out with its names of cities
Our minds to be where we are not,
Our pain to be other than our own:
The time, a bit aside from any
Point we did intend to make,
Crushes our conversation with
Its cruder moral argument. The time,
Like a delator, denounces:
Is a spy in the heart. Has its
Intimate horrors (like a schoolmaster
Denouncing masturbation), assures us
If we take our eyes for a second
Off the ball, we shall soon turn
Into Hitler or De Sade. It has
So many knives, so many slogans,
So many things to die for—and death
Is not enough, unless you die
For exactly the right slogan—
And considers immoral all
Mere incentives to live. The time
Is sly, malicious, has an evil eye.

A glib and abstract time. I hate
The time; I would desire to
Have time, in time, to live without
The crushing weight of purposes
That say everything must be done
And nothing properly. I would wish...
But those who ride wishes like horses
Find when they come to take their fences
Their bottoms fall with a hard bump
On the cold stone ground.
                                    The time
Demands so much, a nagging woman,
Denouncing our impotence, or else
Our salaries, our hobbies, and our friends,
That we forget its own false promises
And that we should be masters of the time.

Tribute to the Legendary Heroes

What lies in the near path, who sought it in the far,
What lies in the easy, who sought it in the hard:
Who also were fit for talk and fit for action, are
Those who translated the habitual language,
The sentence told at the fireside, admonitions,
Into the general propositions
Founded on the atomic facts. Whose words
Were like a set of pegs, tied with strings
To various empirical realities. The red peg
With the red string, tied to all red things:
The green peg with green string to the leaves
Of that particular green. So the symbolic map,
The pegs in the board, once the strings were removed,
Recalled vividly a childhood's actual universe,
Now this dull presence to our dull attention.
These were they
Who set discourse on one side
And on the other side objects,
And because objects are multifarious and tiresome
Invented a language of discourse only about discourse,
As the tired explorer sits at night with his maps,
The lamp on the table, and night
Damp on the outer window, behind curtains.
These also, discoursing about discourse,
Were freed from the tyranny of initiation:
To them a woman was not desirable,
For the correct way to frame this sentence
Is being a woman implies being desirable,
Or if there is a woman, she is desirable,

And in these cases there were no women;
To the intellect, sentences about sentences,
Manipulated by a few simple rules,
Seemed magic to shout down the world of objects.
So one no longer said,
Hitler takes Vienna,
But sentences mentioning all Hitler's doings
Must mention taking Vienna:
Taking Vienna is one of Hitler's functions
Like making speeches, patting children, frightening Jews:
Being Hitler implies.
The relation of implication of being one or the other,
But not both, simple relations:
As not both free and enslaved, and either
Dead or alive, and pain implies sorrow:
Sentences mentioning sorrow mention pain.

Monologue for a Cairo Evening [4]

(To John Waller)

Love one another. Die. The choice is easy.
Pride, lust and envy, whispering at the bar,
Buy us a last one for the road. The road has
Led us, my friend, exactly where we are...

And all the faces slip and slide before us:
And every voice is thick: and every eye
Is on the clock or on the bill: and every
Drink makes the last road more insistent: die,

Die, says the wind. More numerous than you know
The tombs... But yet the golden tower was there.
We wither with no weather. Yet the impulse
Was sensitive that led us up the stair.

Cairo was full of characters. I shall
Remember Larry stocky against a bar,
The round face and the tartan scarf, looking
Like a jovial commercial traveller,

Talking like the occasional angel who descends
By the ladder of alcohol to the banal rocks
Of the wars we do not start: and cannot justify
But how the psyche cushions all its shocks,

Benign euphoria above the glasses,
A whiff of whiskey and a melody,
Vanishing up into another country:
O, what rough beast crawls to the Embassy?

Leaving a plot for a story: leaving a shocker
To sell for sixpence at the chemist's stores,
Describing six neuroses at six a penny
Seeking in one labyrinth six minotaurs...

The flowers that grew out of my brandy-glass
Were all a gully-gully trick. The faces
That looked at me with sideways sliding eyes
The bar's perspective kept within their places.

I shall remember, John, your merciless hail
Of words, a florid weather devil, stripping
The oily outer vine-leaves of my skin
From the soft inner substance of my weeping.

I shall remember the dead: lights, lights
Among the trees and shadows for Kay who is gone
Wafted by laughter for her rendezvous
With jagged marble in her natal London,

And Keith Douglas's shrewd and rustic eyes
That had endured 'the entry of a demon':
His poems spat out shrapnel; and he lies
Where all night long the Narrow Seas are screaming,

And the faces of dead-alive soldiers, a turnip frost
In a grey field, the eyes frozen as if
Brilliantine had licked them to their faces
As it licks down the Sergeant-Major's quiff,

And also the living: Erik swinging from a tree
With impossibly long arms, like a gibbon;
Peter exploring hotel balconies:
Alan unrolling his pink gossip like ribbon,

Sure that this line is just what Modom wants:
In Fleet Street's great bazaar a shopwalker
Who knows the shelves are piled with bales and bales
Of funny stories about Hannen Swaffer,

Or a Berberine bootboy with hyacinthine eyes,
Or Denis with his joggling monocle,
Or Cyril with his frozen one, Medusa,
Medusa to the grey and mediocre;

Or the clear thin voice of Tatiana asking
Its simple, impossible, and ideal questions
Whether indeed there exists above the mellay
A tower of justice: or have you suggestions?

It does not add up to a story or a theory.
It is the gossip-column of the heart.
And yet the nights pass smoothly. And the bar-propped
Exile has lost the courage to depart...

Call it corruption. The corruption is
That we're alone with our impersonations
And though the coin rings dud, no barman cares
To bite the nickel of our valuations

And spit it back upon the counter. Life
In Cairo's possible because we say:
'You are a poet, or a wit, or beauty.
Choose from the wardrobe mistress. We will play.'

Who are the valuable and who the false?
Who are the snobs, and who the bores? And who
Among projectors on this floating island
Is such an honest Gulliver as you,

Old friend, who being simple and merciless
And kind and subtle, can enjoy a show
Where every part's pat in your repertory:
Crude Caliban to priggish Prospero!

To you I dedicate this inconclusive
Conclusion to an unmethodical
Method of being the mass and the observer:
To you, the critical, this curtain call

Of all these painted and tormented faces
And all these squabblings in the dressing-rooms
And all that great death in another country:
More numerous than you know, they lie, the tombs.

'Christ stinks of torture...' But our slippery life
Goes down that funnel too. And Europe stinks
Of the perverted human will, is tortured
Just as our guts are tortured by our drinks.

And Europe spews up Europe, as we spew
Cairo on Cairo; Europe crawls to bed
As Cairenes totter from the crying jag
With half of history throbbing in the head.

And if I write to you, who are the braver
And whom time's complicated madness has
Caught in no intellectual nets, it is that
Some happy facts elude some tragic laws,

Some impulse may be sensitive, some casual
Word may dissolve some envy and some hate,
Some inconsistent are some kind, some luck may
Show more truth than some premeditate,

Some so among these faces. Some who touched us
May help us through a night we cannot touch
Or see, to avoid the tombs, to know the answer:
Whether we loved too little or too much,

Whether the wish for death that comes upon me
In a pale room, on a constricted bed
Needs only sea and sun for dissipation
And the gold slumber of another head,

Among so many, on the sand beside me;
The sea's insistent washing of the sand,
The adolescent silences, the yawnings
The body and the spirit understand,

Or must I go the rocky way, with bleeding
Feet in the night, my knees on the cold floor
Making the penance for inclusive life
To that Exclusive Death above the door,

Christ on his crucifix, who died in this
Region of distances and dust and flies,
Of the cruel rich man and the crippled beggar:
Killed in a country of no compromise.

Some sensitive impulse still alive in us
Some help. Man, intellectual animal,
Weeps in his brilliant darkness. He will cry.
And in the darkness some will hear his call.

Elegy for Adolescent Sex

Always my lust in dreams sought shadows, grey
Boys of the slums and dancers of the screen;
The furtive impulse took its backstreet way;
The little lights were glittering and obscene.

Ghost of a tall girl, gawky like a boy,
O pale slum boy, of my street-corner game;
O sad child crying for your broken toy;
Your shadowy pathos haunts my dream with shame.

114

You come like coughing. Like the sudden whiffs
Of beer and sawdust from the barroom door;
Like white hysteria in handkerchiefs;
Like the cage open, and the lion's roar...

The cosy pathos; girls in combinations
Sipping their cocoa by the blue gas stove;
And schoolboys with their desperate imitations
Under the desk of adult acts of love!

Sex's marine machinery; the call
Of the grim gantry to desire and fear:
A dream all gaslight and all ebbtide, all
A tarry wharfage and a jutting pier!

Alas, incongruous images, remember
The thousand flashlight photographs of lust!
A dry hand crushed a dress, it is December;
Scrawled dirty drawings, it's an attic's dust.

My childhood weeps; a lonely and obscene
Sorrow, transfigured by her diamond hours,
And I am scholarly and seventeen
And petal after petal I tear flowers

And drop them in the water; a flirtation
With how the dandy can be true and love
And the reporter baffle expectation:
White on the stream the ordered petals move.

O ordered flowers: there was the love, the image
Of the rare beauty or the marvellous friend,
The almost crystallising talk...the damage
Done, and the poem weakening at the end.

God still in heaven with his note of query,
And Lenin's margins scored with notes of doubt,
I lie awake and read till I am weary:
But in the dark these shadows crowd about.

I think of all the years that made me expert
In all the things I did not wish to do:
And I would, O pathetic shadow, extort
An advent in the flesh at last from you.

A Bought Embrace

Holding the naked body I had bought
Half gingerly, my chin upon her shoulder,
And gently shuddering in her arms, I thought:
'We choose the easier way as we grow older.

'Ten minutes till the cinema begins,
And time to still the hollow vessel's grief,
Buy off the dream of sorrow; all my sins
Shock easily upon this cushioned reef,

'And all desires seem captious and remote:
On a calm swell, without the grief of wishing,
I bob in sunlight with my little boat,
And hardly notice where my thoughts are fishing...

'What could they dredge from all that sea, but love?
Those I desired and laid my hands upon:
Those me desiring whom they could not move:
And those desired, but not by me touched, gone.

'What matters, whom I wrote my sonnets to,
Whose letters hurt me, who disturbed my dreams?
I do not think I find them here in you.
I find myself, which matters more, it seems.

'I do not think my shillings buy your love.
What should she care about her customer,
Who knows, whatever he is thinking of,
He is not thinking specially of her?

And yet I think you do not wish me ill,
So unexacting in your arms I lie,
So gently leave the voyage to your will,
Till the craft capsize and the steersman die...

'Why think, indeed? The body knows the story:
A single shudder brings the boat to wreck.
Purged of all ecstasies, I feel no more...I
Lightly with dry lips brush your placid neck.'

Metaphysical Epistle (A fragment) [5]

(To Lawrence Durrell)

All causes, for Plotinus, were
Contained within the great Because.
Climb that interminable stair
And look with fear to where it was.
Look from the height above the storm
Where the Ideal absorbs the Form.

And far below the Logos took
Chimeric shakes, defined the soul,
Distortion of th'impassive look
Where the Intelligibles roll.
Where the spermatic Concepts lie
With promise of Plurality.

For even the dual Intelligence
Is still an object to itself.
Keys to the lexicons of sense
Lie all too handy on its shelf.
It knows itself, but still that void
Creates a world to be enjoyed.

The *I* that knows the *me* is not
The *me* it knows, the emptiest *me,*
Its mere awareness has begot
A something else that claims to be;
From such divisions must descend
Angels, and angels, with no end.

So of three Hypostases, two
Had Ousia, the last had none.
We know the One is not the Two.
We cannot say it is the One.
And all depends on Unity
That cannot either Think or Be.

Yet what diaspora is left
If from this Nothing we depart,
Sense of centrality bereft,
An Appetite, and Head, and Heart,
And all the broken glass recalls
A war of warring animals?

The *All* is an illusion, and
A *Nothing* needs, to be a world:
A flag that is not, by a hand
Phantasmal, in a void unfurled.
Nothing is *Nothing,* alas...

An Evening Half of Fog

An evening half of fog in London
A rascal boy resembling
My loved one came to my encounter
And the look he flung me made
Me lower my eyes with modesty

I trailed this bad type far along,
Hands in his pocket, whistling,
We seemed between the houses as
An open wave of the Red Sea
He the Hebrews, Pharaoh me

Let these waves of red bricks fall
If you were not the well-beloved
I am the sovereign of Egypt
His sister-spouse and his army
If you are not the unique love

The turning of a burning road
With all the fires of its facades
Wounds of the fog exuding blood
And the façades lamenting a
Woman who resembled him

It was his look of a nonhuman
The cicatrice on his bare neck
That emerged tipsy from the tavern
The moment that I recognised
The falsity of love itself

When he had come back at last
To his country wise Ulysses
His old dog remembered him...

The Streets of Cairo

The streets of Cairo now
        Call with too many colours
In all their beggars' voices;

And broken lights allow
        Sorrows to flow like odours
From the ambiguous houses.

Framed in the dark the green
        Windows of a café
And the brown eating faces

Dumb as the things they mean
        Are bent over coffee
Tying the mind's laces

With clumsy and hopeless fingers;
        I am reminded of beggars
And their insistent hands.

And a jasmin odour lingers
        Among the spices and sugars
The City understands.

An Elegy for Keith Bullen

*(Headmaster of Gezira Preparatory School, Cairo, and a friend
to English poetry and poets)*

A great room and a bowl full of roses,
Red roses, a man as round as a ripe rose,
Lying in a bowl of sun. And who supposes
Such a sad weight could support such a gay pose.

Flying his sad weight like a round baby's
Petulant balloon! He has blue pebbles for eyes,
Petulant, bewildered, innocent eyes like a baby's;
Like a great baby or a clipped rose he lies

In a white bowl of light in my memory;
And expands his tenuous sweetness like a balloon;
I shall die of feeling his dear absurdity
So near me now, if I cannot cry soon.

Keith was particularly Sunday morning,
Red roses, old brandy, was unharrying Time,
Was that white light, our youth; or was the fawning
Zephyr that bobs the gay balloon of rhyme,

He bobbed incredibly in our modern air;
With his loose jacket, his white panama hat,
As he leaned on his walking stick on the stone stair
He seemed a balloon, moored down to the ground by that.

As he leaned at the bar and ordered us pink gin
Or arranged a flutter on the three-fifteen
He seemed a child, incapable of sin:
We never knew him prudent, cold, or mean.

Or tied to the way the world works at all
(Not even tied enough for poetry);
All that he was we only may recall,
An innocent that guilt would wish to be,

A kind, a careless, and a generous,
An unselfseeking in his love of art,
A jolly in his great explosive fuss;
O plethora of roses, O great heart!

Elegy

The waxen and the false grace of tulips,
The scentless heads in many drawing-rooms,

Pursues what I write, like the piano-note,
The velvet dress and the cake crumbs,

And the path sweeping up the mossy
Lawns, impoverished by great trees,
And the conservatory's tomato-plants
And all my idle and infertile days:

And you to whom I remain an evil enigma
Remember pleasantly the white of birds
Against the old quad's green, remember
How friendship for us was not upon the cards.

Remember your old coats, your golf umbrella,
Your loud laughter, growth of thought and taste:
And me, in whom your sweet civility
Found only barren soil, a churlish waste.

O lady, had I speech as I have words
And had I love as I have images...
Think of me silent, awkward, blind,
And wait until the world is at my knees,

I may be pleasant then! Poor egoist
With this one gift, and could but be at ease
With you who might have saved me from my poetry,
Who offered life, instead of lonely days.

Aubade

(For Paddy)

Lying here early, we smile at our love,
At the calm day closing of night's great gulfs,
At the sheets so dimpled and smug above
The deep drowned bodies they do not think of:
And who would now think that these waves were wolves,

That last night your body beneath the sheets
With its piston legs and serpent arms
Was a treacherous sea, and cradled fleets
Of great spice galleons through tropic heats—
Sunk with their poppy and all their charms!

Awake! Awake, young woman, in a mild air.
There's a clinging and a soft rain like silk
Outside our window. Sweet one spread your hair,
Rough with sea salt, on a pillow where
Your neck and shoulders are my morning milk.

The geese and the turkeys are cackling now;
The kitchen scudge is scrubbing at the pot;
That deep sad yawning is a pensive cow;
And we ourselves may wonder how
Into this lucky land we ever got.

With its beer that smacks of the sawdust floor
And the hearty spit of the local types,
And its eloquent lobsters that crawl ashore
Begging the diner to ask for some more,
And its tenpenny whiskeys that cheer the tripes!

Country of open bowels and open hearts!
Here steaks are red and raw like carter's fists!
Potatoes, great and mealy; cream-drenched tarts!
We eat, we drink, we sleep. By fits and starts
We note a theme and how the theme persists.

For Eliot's Sixtieth Birthday

All came to pieces in my hands,
The hesitant and the humane,
A history as flat as prose
Soiled by the salt poetic stain,

All darkness, but the burning rose,
All hesitation, but the dance,
All human love, that habit turned
To lust, to hate, to glum routine,

The last few liberals advance,
Define what their restrictions mean,

The bomb fell and the city burned
And with my palms I sifted sands:

All his ingenious fancy knows:
The horror of the human scope,
That turns from its fallacious hope,
All ashes to the burning rose.

Loose these intellectual knots:
A crumbling yellow page of prose,
Murders, massacres, and plots.
Salty pillars round the plain;
Redemption through the flaming rose;
And memory the lovely stain
By which the damned his blessing knows.

Poems from
Leaves without a Tree
1953

Leaves without a Tree was published by The Hokuseido Press in Tokyo in 1953. All the poems in this volume had been included in *The Traveller has Regrets* (1948), with the exception of the three which follow: 'An Elegy for Stefan Schimanski', 'To a Lady' and 'Sakurajima (Japan)'.

An Elegy for Stefan Schimanski

(Man of letters, editor, war correspondent, my good friend, drowned when his transport plane crashed in the sea early in the Korean campaign)

The watcher's seat precedes the newsreel skies.
Headlong to headlines, fallen like a stone,
One wild, and worried, and persistent, dies
Much, at a pinch, like men of harder bone.

Sunk in a sea's insidious extent
Less deep, less wide, than man's destructive will—
Such killing cold would not for him relent
Whose heart was never cold, nor poised to kill,

Not like the hawk, nor like the hooded airman
But a mild seeker for a lost kind God,
A literary scout, a sort of chairman
For groups of bothered notions! And how odd

He should end so, and inappropriateness
Of the steel context! Definitely dead
Like any hero, Stefan seems the less
What one remembers more—the shy cocked head,

As I have seen it often on evenings at home,
Turning aside from its talk of the latest book,
To where some Venus, breaking through the foam
Of cocktail chatter, had transfixed its look,

Springing above the crowded heads between,
Some flushed young face with conscious beauty fired,
Like, on a burnt brown hill, one shoot of green:
And Stefan, with a sighing hope, admired!

Has lost all girls for good now. May have found,
One prays, beyond our plummeting, his peace
Upon the bosom of that deepest ground
That is our only, or our last release.

To a Lady

You, familiar and remote,
At your ease you keep your distance,
At your distance you keep your ease,
And can deal with the insistence
Of the lover at your knees
Beauty catches by the throat:
You, familiar and remote!

Beauty catches by the throat
You, familiar and remote!

Beauty catches by the throat
When a look postpones a pleasure
For the pleasure of a look
Into eyes that take the measure
Of the wriggler on their hook
Between the water and the boat:
Beauty catches by the throat!

Between the water and the boat
Beauty catches by the throat!

Between the water and the boat
Let your fish back in the water
Back in the water let him fish:
And is that kindness, beauty's daughter?
Was he not worthy of your dish
Or did you know his kind by rote:
Between the water and the boat!

Or did you know his kind by rote
Between the water and the boat?

Sakurijima (Japan)

(A volcano)

A broken summit under sagging clouds:
Earth-steam that drifts to merge with vaporous air
And, like a jungle's pendant foliage, shrouds
The wild beast sleeping in this rocky lair.

His name is Fire. Famished, he lurks alone.
His stout cave walls to sullen skies incline,
Their aspiration, to a perfect cone,
Cut cruelly by the crater's lateral line.

Still as a painting now, these austere slopes
Have seen this beast-god gulp up soil and houses,
Whose long tongue licks to swallow human hopes
When, drunk with his own anger, he carouses.

But this archaic god could not daunt men:
The villagers went back to build again.

Other Poems of the 1950s

Prayers for the New Year [6]

Heart, poise for a moment, hollow of purpose,
Like a high bird over the turning year
Or, high swan heart, be lost in the hoar sky
While I fashion a bleak poem with frosty fingers
And strew what blessing I can on a bloody year
And turn my own life's drift to a thought of purpose.

The war and rage of our world are a rude winter
And we warm our hands at the small fires of a heart
Half-choked, poor heart, with unraked ash of sin
I rake among now, but with clumsy fingers,
Or blow upon, to coax out of the heart
Some purity of warmth against the winter.

And if, for a moment, the flame like a bird rises
Over the page, yet I know the shape of a poem
Is other and better than the shape of a life
Not shaped, as a poem is shaped with deft fingers,
And I seek in my own life for more than a poem
If ever prayer, O purer fire-bird! rises

Into that infinite sky which is our image
Of God's great mercy that we so misuse:
Of all the graces, signs, and premonitions
That we let slip so slackly through our fingers.
Lord, all thy mercy though I still misuse,
Heal whole at last this heart, thy broken image!

The Praise of Spring

It's spring again, I frame it from my window,
And like small spots of cuckoo-spit the buds
Thick on thin branches by the bricky wall
Suggest a life deposited, not growing,
Or a young hope that has not faced it all,

Though there, beyond the placid sacred oblong
Of frost-chapped grass around Moravian bones,
The biscuit shafts of workers' flats shoot high,
Seasonable emblems also of renewal,
And there sand-heaps and concrete-mixers lie,

And there in morning-walks I halt my children
And from the rubble watch the theorem rise,
Out of that nursery floor bombs left, to prove
That mathematics underprops the homely
And calculation is the scope of love,

And so this spring I shall not praise the potplants,
The curled proud hyacinth, droopt daffodil,
But praise fresh paint upon the Chelsea doors,
Girls by the Old King's Head in new print dresses,
And scouring housewives at their doorstep chores,

For if our architecture is organic,
Our proud street-muddle like our mass of verse,
Our ways of doing things, that somehow work,
We must ourselves create a conscious springtime
Nor peer where bits of vegetation lurk

Forgetting we are living, dying, also,
In a more tense and complicated way
Than any leaf or little London bird;
Or, if the buds and chirpings are a message;
They are a message only we have heard

And coded in our own and different language
To cheer ourselves to an ambiguous task
By juxtaposing chimney-pots and parks,
And praising life, but also praising masters,
The great who made the obvious remarks.

So spring is like the shift from mild to bitter,
From winter overcoats to gaberdine,
From reading Gibbon to re-reading Blake.
The deep source is not blasphemed by the fountains
At play above the artificial lake.

Little Lament [7]

(For Nicoline Goodman)

O time of terrible elegies,
I turn aside and weep
For what, though distant while I wake,
Disdains to haunt my sleep,

An insolence of centuries
Gathered about a head
Whose pose mere transience does not break
Nor crumble with the dead,

High head, its look now turned away
Towards another scene,
That even when transient seemed to know
What all the sybils mean,

And seemed to dominate our day,
A castle of the plains,
As grey as mist, as cold as snow,
As endless as the rains,

The look of horsemen who prevailed
Against the nomad spears,
The music of an ancestry,
And vain must be my tears

For one to whom the heart availed,
Whose courage was so high
That even in an elegy
I cannot meet her eye.

On the Playground

(For Edwin Muir)

Having collected poets like cigarette cards,
I am ready enough, now, on the noisy playground
To swap so many of my crumpled treasures for
Conkers, foreign stamps, a lucky penny.

So many of my best proved Cretan liars:
'Observe my churlishness, it shows my heart':
'My poster-shriekings are a care for language':
'I fight on every side, and am sincere!'

And the mere patience of your following
A dream's faint clue that, closed with, can convey
The winding clutch of labyrinth or coastline,
Your dogged life, that exercise in focus,

Seem dull enough to many. Why not crack up,
Yell, make faces, swagger like a wide boy?
Your stance has an archaic dignity:
What use, today, an art that distances?

Conscripted to this uncongenial century
For peasant and for philosophical virtues,
Sturdy, mild poet, it is your distinction
To wear dumb goodness as a speaking style.

We other learners, complicating surfaces,
Muff our responses. You ring baldly true.
May the bad dream, broken in the middle, not recur:
And may your autumn be relaxed and lucky!

For R. P. Blackmur

(In memory of taking the chair for him at the Institute of Contemporary Arts)

Blackmur, whose cloudy pregnancies,
Scanning low skies, I vainly strove
To body to Junonian ease
And fit for Ixion or for Jove,

In Dover Street thick darkness spread,
Yet goddess-thewed in many a phrase:
Oracular that riddling head,
A Spartan broth for I.C.A.s.

Yet, back in Chelsea, at your ease,
And kind to the presumptuous young,
Words that could both persuade and please
Dropped lightly from a liberal tongue.

The great creative puzzlers pass,
And we who serve them pass as well;
What is the trick to say alas
In tones that will be audible?

Time passes, memory blurs, I find
I have forgotten voice and look:
But the dense treasures stay, unmined:
Clay, nuggets, diamonds of your book.

To a Muse seeking a Muse

(For Anne Ridler)

Time is a shadowy wood
Gaps in whose thickets show
Once in a lifetime, twice,
The country that we know,
Its granaries of good,
But twists then in a trice
Our path to hide the glimpse
Of the calm, candid face,
Guessed image of a voice,
Countering the chattering imps
Of lower woodland ways,
And all the cares that cark,
That in our stumbling dark
Cries grave and gray: 'Rejoice,
O wayward wanderer,
Rejoice that all things are
Lost path and thorny brake,
And high unlucky star!'

You were that voice to me,
Guessed at and yet unknown:
When what was heard was shown
There was congruity.
Caught in no witch's cape,
I saw no sorceress there
But saw the comely shape
Of human sympathy:
Kempt, and unmaenad hair,
Yet saw sweet wildness touch
My listening woodland folk,
Enchantress sweet and pure,
Till they rejoiced so much
They cannot yet be sure
They saw you, heard you speak,
But in a dream that broke
When all was still to seek.

What use our craft, except
Time we can intercept
And grip it to a point
Where breakings heal? Oh, but
The Time is out of joint,
Or in a dying rut,
But not in you. So cry
Loud for your heavenly Muse!

What was too humble in that sigh,
Unwayward wanderer,
Should one who long had sought for her
Under the multiplicity
Of shiftings of the sacred tree,
Too harshly disabuse?

Poetic Generations [8]

When first I thrummed the lyre
Right at the back of the stage,
O what politic fire
Inspired our vocal rage!
Our feet could not keep still
For the shuffling beat of the drum,
Our prophets all cried, 'Kill
Corrupt Byzantium!'
But when that war broke out
And all of us sailed away
An ache in the heart bred doubt
At the sight of the world's decay.

The bards we'd left behind us
When we went overseas
Were seeking then to bind us
In a net of images;
Water had drowned their valley,
Words, fished up in a welter,
Were set in their bowling-alley
To scatter helter-skelter.
We turned away as scorning
The deep sea of their dreams;
Dreams are a bore in the morning,
Or so in the morning it seems.

Companion at the bar,
The shooting days are over!
I wonder who you are.
Where is the Muse, my lover?
Who has her light, he hoards it:
And shaken with what rage
Did I dream once of words that
Would burn up my page?
The new brisk young approach us,
The born disabused:
With hard tight eyes reproach us
For coins and ease misused.

We are not the last or the first
With silly tears to cry
For never losing the thirst
We cannot satisfy.
If this is not what I mean,
It is almost what I meant:
We must make the instruments clean
As the predicament,
We must put ourselves to school
In sullen middle age
Till compass, square, and rule
Restore the vocal rage!

Mannerist Poem

Images of tears induce
          actual tears, and rhetoric
A kind of ghost gesture:
                    talk of bodies,
how they moved and with what beauty,
will not bring them back again.

That young woman leaned forward,
                    her throat was dented, her
bones all fine and small,
                    her blue silk slipped off
a terracotta shoulder, showing
the top half of tanned breasts
sheathed in glassy linen, stiff
as the angular and hieratic
gesture with which she lifted
her small glass of Noilly Prat;
the lemon rind bobbing on it
did not touch the edge.

'Privation, matter, motion,
by these from the height of the understanding
physical things fall away.'

She sat wedged sideways in
an armchair, her legs up and
wide over, and a blue shadow
or a blue mystery
swimming between. Open sandals,
long toes, a supple stretching.
The nails, of course, bright red.

(And what could be emptier than
the relations of mathematics?

Or more full of awe than
the glimpses beyond understanding
that fold the mind back on itself
like an unwritten page?)

And not alone in the chair
she lent herself with a certain
good-natured detachment
to the solicitations of
an artist from lost Vienna:
whose lust itself was pathos.
As I grow older
I observe such occasions
With more of an abstract eye.

Epigrams:

BEDSIDE STORY

(after the French of Robert Graves)

With, at each elbow, one fine woman,
The male is more or less than human
And, from compunctious tenderness,
Turns first to her he likes the less.

The female, on the other hand,
With two strong men at her command,
Though nice, finds chivalry a bore
And first plucks him she fancies more.

THE LADY TO HER LOOKING GLASS

My eyes are dry. Tears will not flow.
My contact lenses too must go.
My skin that always held a faint
Magnolia lustre cakes like paint.
Dry heat wilts petals. Lock the house,
My dry and undemanding spouse.

THE SOLDIER AND THE ARTIST

Great Captains spot the truth and tell:
'He drinks, he's dirty, there's a smell...
There's *something* wrong about this chap!...
Of women. Did he once get clap?'

He was a great wrecked galleon, yes:
The soldier was a safe success.
Their craft collided over Styx.
The Man of War was knocked for six.

Note: From an anecdote of Douglas Cooper's about Field Marshal
Montgomery's dislike of Augustus John.

The Poet on his Birthday [9]

All came to pieces in my hands,
The hesitant and the humane,
A history as flat as prose
Soiled by the salt poetic stain.

The bomb fell and the city burned
And with my palms I sifted sands
And I am paid what I have earned.

All darkness round the burning rose,
All hesitation through the dance,
All human love that habit turned
(O waters of mirage, advance!)

To lust, to hate, to glum routine
From what was ardour in the glance
Define what my restrictions mean.

All, my ingenious fancy knows:
The horror of the human scope
That turns from its fallacious hope,
All ashes, to the burning rose.

Loose these intellectual knots:
A crumbling yellow page of prose:
Murders, massacres, and plots.

Salty pillars round the plain.
Redemption through the flaming rose.
And memory the lovely stain
By which the damned his blessing knows.

Image and Person

First love what God had made. A bird flies past
But now must love what you have made of that,
The mask you made in acting out a play;
I must leave fantasy, and love the real,
Or leave God's real, and love your fantasy;
A face as wrinkled as an actress's,
Another woman's voice laid on your own,
Layer upon layer of self-importances,
Of knowing better and of being wise:
A ravaged gesture as of broken rock
How many seas, now mine, had beaten on!
Still with proud nostrils, O my wooden horse,
With rolling eyes, round as a rocking horse's:
I shall not, poor child, have another ride!

A bird flies past. The sky is empty. I
Am tongue-tied in your special sort of drama,
Past the rehearsals of the nursery;
I am not sure I like your dialogue.
I cannot trace your image through your mask.
And is what breaks within me my own heart?
Or a false image I, not God, had made?
What cracks and crumbles, is it me or you?
A bird flies past, the awful sky is empty.

Conditions
1969

Conditions was first published by The Byron Press, Nottingham, in 1969. All the poems from *Conditions* are included below except 'A Poem about Love', which originally formed Section 3 of 'Three Poems about Love' in *The Traveller has Regrets,* and appears thus in the present collection.

For my Wife on her Fiftieth Birthday

A little time is fifty years
For so much joy,
              so many tears,

Nor fifty summers were too long
For every summer
              was a song

That echoed through
              the winter's cold
And but one tale the burden told:

She shall have labour, pain, and woe,
She shall bring love
              where'er she go.

Snow, rain and sun of all her hours
Shall shine among her loves
              like flowers

That are not flowers of a day.
O how they shine
              and not decay!

So let us gather roses now
To deck a
        matron Muse's brow,

Slim on her stem, herself a rose.

How time stands still now, so time flows!

The Human Situation

Between presumption and despair
Climb upon the narrow stair
Of the proper human scope:
Do not hope for safety, but
At the worst remember that
None are saved who lose their hope.

All are lost, though, who, too much,
Presume upon a winning touch
Or imagine that the sky
Looks on the peculiar sins
Of the man who always wins
With a mild forgiving eye.

If the times are bad, of course
They have been, and will be, worse,
Will be, have been, better, too
Yet, though that makes abstract sense,
Practical indifference
Simply will not, will not, do.

For, tossing on a stormy sea,
What is it to you or me
That the sea is sometimes calm?
Thinking of a better time
Or depicting it in rhyme
Will not ease a present harm.

That is true. But truer still
That to purify the will
We must think of evil as
Something other than the weather,
We ourselves have worked together
To make it what it is and was.

Heavy, heavy though it be
Our responsibility
It is a better lot than if
We should set out from the shore
With no sail, and with no oar,
And with no steerboard to our skiff.

Nature is a goddess who
Has no thought for me or you
Other than as vehicles
For the angry seeds of life,
Antagonistic love and strife,
So abundantly she spills.

Yet, of course, we love her still,
Turning from her makes us ill,
Even I who sermonise
Walk (by nature) in her ways,
Count such charms as gild my days
By the fire of female eyes.

And the mere philosopher
Turning in disgust from her,
From this Circe and her cave,
Lacks a certain chthonic fire
Of unsatisfied desire
That makes men fools but makes them brave.

Nature, though, is not enough,
Made of mixed and striving stuff
Like wine that fires and floods our wits.
Pity the wholly sober man;
Also the human drinking can;
Our bouts should have their starts and fits.

And it is fitting, on the whole,
To think as nobly of the soul
As its uneasy case permits,
Its being in a situation
Where someone of superior station
Finds much that jars and much that grits;

Cartesius' ghost-in-the-machine
Expresses crudely what I mean,
Better is Plato's metaphor,
That of a flagon with a thirst
Which, still replenished, cannot burst,
So fast it leaks upon the floor:

For say that we could day and night
Pander to each appetite,
Pack our time with panther hours,
Still that case, as Butler saw,
Rests on an intrinsic flaw —
Their satisfaction is not ours.

And (hedonism no solution
Since it leads to dissolution
Of a central core of strength
In the rational loving will),
Twist and turn we may, but still
Must take ourselves in hand at length.

Nothing could be flatter than
Such a trig account of man
In the plain didactic mode,
Such accounts are needed, though,
If our travelling human show
Is to keep upon the road.

If when fast cars skid and swerve,
Drivers most must keep their nerve,
We, and now, must most keep ours;
And a statement of that case
Though it lack the lyric grace
Never asked for any flowers.

Yes, the case is what it is.
There is dignity in this,
In choosing to be not deceived.
And it is what it is not.
For we find that, taking thought,
We also act what we conceived.

Language has its uses then
In differentiating men
From less anxious animals,
In transforming outer fate
Into what we think and state
And crumbling down the fatal walls.

Mortal and appetitive
On these ramparts we must live
And seek our narrow safety out,
Safety built on danger, for
All peace implies a hidden war
And all belief is based on doubt.

Men are dying as I write
In the Asiatic night,
Not a word I write will help,
Stanch or soothe a single wound,
Stop a single cannon's round,
Still a single jackal's yelp.

For, buttering no parsnips, and
Neither, on the other hand,
Breaking any bones, words are
Harmless or useless, as you care
To put it; and unwanted where
Mars drives with rage his crashing car—

Words of this sort! Our fever asks
For hollow words from hollow masks
To stimulate to active rage;
The words of headlines or of speeches,
The wind dressed up in coat and breeches
And prancing on the leader page!

But these help less. For nourished by
Rank wind, our poor sheep rot and die,
And our bad shepherds shirk the blame
And change their coats from week to week:
But the more colourings they seek
The more the poison is the same.

For seeking to be quite secure
Against all odds, these fools endure
For their reward, the awful sense
That the vile ogre's mask they face
With hate, too soon will shift its place
Onto their own side of the fence.

The case for the poetic word
Is not, then, perfectly absurd;
It is against self-righteous rant
And ever-broken promises
That a slow argument like this
May fill a really long-felt want.

I promise nothing. But I say
That we can know a better way
And may have grace to follow it;
We know the worst ways just as well
And there's no sinner in deep hell
On whom we have the right to spit.

We cannot promise, but can pray
For help upon the human way
From hate and error quiet release:
The calming of our vain desires,
And patience in the purging fires,
And in the human city peace.

Speech of a Sufferer

No, of course, one doesn't like to go over it
But of course one does, and perhaps going over it
In words sometimes to somebody like you
Not particularly involved but inquisitive,
Though there is malice in all curiosity,
In all interest even a spice of malice —
A friend's weakness is one's own strength —
And only lack of malice in pure concern
Which saints may feel but only prigs pretend to,
Perhaps going over it, as I was going to say,
If it doesn't help much, might not very much harm
And might make it clear in a way how very unclear
What there is to go over is. Have a cigarette.

Well, you know how it started, of course, the actual fact.
I was already in a pretty unbalanced state
When I jumped from that train. How much, up to then,
You would call real is, for me, quite a question.
And I ought to have died, of course. But I got up.
There was a very tall man waiting for me.
I was naked and bleeding. He was bluff and jovial,
Hospitable, you might say. I remember his words:
'Come into my house, and my dogs will eat you up'.
He might have been Death. He sounded more like Sin.
I didn't like him though I felt I knew him.
I turned away to other archetypes,
Through a field of corn, towards a dark wood,
But then lay down in a little crater of earth,
I had not reached the wood; and in fact I wasn't
Anywhere like that. I pulled myself together,
Knocked on one of their wooden cottage doors.
They found a local doctor to stitch me up,
I remember him, working like a cobbler.
The very peculiar thing, a bad bump,
From a moving train, wrists and throat bleeding,
But I don't remember feeling any pain.
At the moment of death, you are supposed to hear
God's Yes or his No. Had they got the signals wrong?
I heard a great boom out of the sky condemning me,
And remember muttering a protest, or a prayer,
Claim to be a special case perhaps. Have a drink.

And then of course it was voices all the way,
Voices and shocks, hallucinatory voices
Of old friends telling me what they really thought of me
Or what I really ought to think of myself,
And what I was in for, lots of unpleasantness,
Whether I did live, or I did die.
They seem external, until at length one finds
One can push about and pattern what they are saying,
They are parts of oneself, to play with in one's head.
I hope so, anyway. Refill your glass.

There were kinder voices, calling me back to my journey,
Or I hope kinder. One always hopes, one's friends do,
A real crash might turn one into a saint.
One's old habits reform very quickly:
It was almost the same journey over again,
Journey of hope, and fear, and hesitation,
Succumbing to many temptations, resisting some,
And oddly enough the important moments still
The ones where the stock responses don't work
And even the subtle skills are out of place.
I don't think illness proves anything about God.
Praying helps sometimes, but it might be a lot safer
Never to have thought about grace or hell or heaven
But just to be a decent liberal, with moderate standards,
Such people stick to the rails. And poetry
Helps a bit, I suppose, but too much imagination
Is as much of a snare as a help. I remember
Green, mostly, green through dusty bars, and how
Everything turns symbolic in a corny way:
Looking at pigeons through the hospital window,
Very beautiful, swirling in the sun,
And a fellow patient asks sardonically:
'Well, do you think that pigeons live for ever?'
Twice, too, I remember someone calling my attention
To a little bird, a lame one, just escaping
From a waiting cat: a sort of lingua franca
Perhaps of people who have just gone over the edge —
The cat our fleshly lusts, the bird the soul?
But I've always loved cats, and cats must eat.
You get insights but they don't work out as logic.

Oh, if you want something a little more poetical,
I used to think my wife was in another room,
In the female ward, putting out a hopeless hand to me.
And I thought my wishes had a magic power,
Bringing about earthquakes or revolutions,
For which I felt afterwards most, most remorseful.
Alone against the fiend? Perhaps I was him,
All grief and sloth. Or was it he who watched me,
Made me walk backwards and against the clock,
And warned against the poverty of seasons?

Was there some evil secret never spoken,
Because to speak it well might make it true?
The garden in the autumn gathered dust
But still seemed lovely through my dusty window.
And yet I never was a gardener.
Come back, some evening, for another drink.

Estrangement

Was it for almost a year?
Late, late in her shabby room
Till the last bus had gone
Night after night her gloom
And never his hand laid on,

Lest she should shrink in fear,
Small breast or boyish thigh
Or short crisp hair that had
First caught his sensual eye:
'People would think us mad

To sit, doing nothing, here',
She would mock. Summer came.
They would seek some shadowy glade
To suit their shadowy game
That never would be played,

And then the leaves grew sere:
'Friends grow past each other.
You wanted us to be friends
Like sister and like brother?
How raggedly it ends!'

If it could have been with a tear!
In his sentimental way
He might have still held hands
Through a lost and hoarded day
Of summer meadowlands,

But the snub, and the cold sneer!
What wish and what constraint
Had taught her tongue to bite
Through his dark leafy plaint
As cuttingly as light,

Her puckering brows to peer
Past facile sympathies
At inner self-regard?
He had willed, on the whole, this:
And this was his reward.

Barrington in 1798 [10]

Wexford had fallen. I traversed that county
To see the ruins occasioned by the war:
Twice-stormed Enniscorthy, broken stone,
And charred: the melancholy relics
Of ten stiff hours of killing at New Ross:
On Vinegar Hill, fresh plump elastic turf
On pits bursting with bodies; a windmill there
Splashed at the top, by turning of the sails,
With blood and brains flung upwards from the bottom
Of victims shot or piked there by the rebels:
Black Enniscorthy court-house, where we burned
Eighty of them alive: at Scullabogue
As black the barn where in retaliation
Above ten dozen Protestants were roasted,
Also alive! Terrific ruins both!

Ruins. I traversed that county. At Gorey
No single house undamaged, and the dead
Only half-covered in the roadside ditches.
A rebel victory that. Our own commander,
A Castle flutterer, a handsome man,
Had never led troops in the field before:
Wishing to see some action, feeling some
Inferiority to the veterans
Who, unlike him, had spent their early lives
Blowing out people's brains, he led his men—
Some cannon, and the Antrim regiment—
Into a defile, where he lost his cannon,
Lost his own brains, and lost his Antrim heroes,
Stuck there with ten-or-twelve-feet pikes: like pigs.

Sic transit gloria mundi! And at Wexford
Three spiked heads stood above the court-room door:
Bagenal Harvey, Colclough, Captain Keogh.
These men were rebels who had suffered justice:
These men were my relations and my friends.
Colclough and Harvey now were mere black lumps:
Keogh's head stood highest, but the eating air
Made no impression on it.

      That proud face
(Most pale indeed, but scarce to be called livid)
Was as in life: eyes open, hair unruffled,
More like a marble head with glassy eyes
Than rotting death. I never met a doctor
Who could explain that. Lake had had them killed.
Hunter commanded now. I spoke to him:
The three heads then were taken down and buried.

But I slept ill, that pale face, these eyes,
Troubled my sleep. Two or three months before
I had dined in Wexford with these rebel leaders,
And others, nearly all of them now dead.
The bottle circulated, there were jokes,
But soon the talk was all about rebellion.
Cunning, about the probabilities,
Its likeliness in an excited time,
Its chances of success: no taking sides.
But say it was successful, who'd be killed?
It was their cautious way to draw men in:
Chaff and old birds: of course, I soon saw through it!

Drinking with unavowed conspirators,
My colleagues, my relations, and my friends,
What should I do? Get up and quit the house
Or give a turn to the conversation?
The last. I turned jestingly to Keogh:
'Now my dear friend, it's clear that you and I
Will be on different sides in this fine business—
And one of us will hang before the end,
I on a lamp-post in the streets of Dublin,
You over water on the bridge at Wexford!
Let's make a bargain. If we beat you, I'll
Do what I can to save you: you save me,
Too, from the honour of the Dublin lamp-post!'

We shook hands on the bargain, and we laughed,
And turned to our wine with better cheer:
But riding home at midnight then I knew
Him or myself a dead man before autumn.
I kept my promise, tried to save his life.
He did resist the rebel butcheries:
And showed humanity. But while I spoke
To Mr Secretary Cooke of this,
He handed me a just-come-in despatch.
Wexford had fallen: and 'to make examples'
Keogh had been hanged upon the bridge at Wexford,
His head cut off, and stuck upon a spike.
What did he look like at that dinner party?
Livid and marble and with glassy eyes?

O what Medusa, to me invisible,
Held at the last and fixed his Irish eyes?

On the Persistence of
Humanity

I often wonder if the race should die:
My restless body and my fuddled mind,
Machine-like work and torpid lethargy;
The self-importance of my fumbling kind;
The filthy cruelty; the waste of words;
The social goodness with its bony thumbs;
The packet recipe for cream and curds,
Pussy watch sparrow, sparrow watch the crumbs!
I think of happy men who work, eat, sleep,
Watch Television, in the quiet night perish;
I think of managers who never weep;
Yet there is something still that I can cherish.
I knew love best in hells of fear and grief;
And love outlasts belief, and disbelief.

I want the bloody human race to run
Over the hurdles of its tinny cars
Until that black star pops, that dying sun
We imitate in our preposterous wars:
Murders, lies, wars! And yet I like my sort,
Because I am the sort of clot they are:
Come Judgment Day, and what is my retort? —
'I loved that session in a public bar:
I loved a pussy, loved a little bird;
One ate the other, in a natural way;
I served up misery in a tasty word;
I never wasn't glad to greet the day.
For all the noisy interfering pain,
Given a chance, I'd run the tape again!'

Fearful of dark, for silliest light I cry:
The bawling sergeant on the barrack square,
The bishop's guff, the advertiser's lie,
The chemist's gloss upon my loved one's hair,
The rigged hoarse cheers at the inane mass meeting,
The tartiest weeklies, their most snide reviews,
Long journeys ending in a brush-off greeting,
The sweet fresh morning and its stale sour news!
Friend beneath enemy, O human face,
And loving enemy behind old friend,
Dear deadpan propping failure and disgrace
And in all endings live, unending end,
Unpardonable, we shall carry on:
And other clots like us, when we are gone.

Human Types

Politics is what people do
Typically, or so say you,
Carrying your head high
Since you are ready to die
For what you know to be not true.

Thinkers have an untypical face,
Shy, hunted, and fugitive,
Since they are ready to live
By the brute facts of the case
And so feel themselves out of place.

And idealists say that what
Looks the case is in fact not.
This gives them a sense of strain
Cancelling out sin or pain.
These types worry a lot.

Poets and truly religious men,
What do these look like then?
Tired, muddled, perhaps kind?
Alive at the edge of the mind?
Hard to type, but one knows when.

Epistle to a Young Poet

And driving once on an October evening
Home from the park, lamps drizzly, and mist
Twining among the trees, I said, 'It grows
Dim and mysterious now'. The little girl,
Looking about, said, 'Where is it mysterious?'
She saw the trees, the lights, the gathering dusk.
I said, 'You say it is mysterious
When you can't see, you wonder what it is'.
She said, 'But where, but show me!' I said then,
'Not anywhere, not like these yellow lamps,
Not like the trees, not even like the mist.
It is a feeling on these autumn evenings,
Being cold and late and wanting to get home,
Seeing the rooms alight behind the curtains,
Wondering who the people are behind the curtains,
Or how the park grows lost behind the trees,
A feeling very much like loneliness;
Seeing things different, wanting to explore'.
She said, 'But where is it mysterious?:
And it would be the same if one explored.

The park is shut at five. One could step over,
Drag feet through dank grass, to the Serpentine,
Guess at lost swans upon the darkened water,
Sitting on a sopping bench, and brood a poem,
And it would be essentially the same
As when in summer we drank beer, ate ices,
The children brought stale bread to feed the ducks;
The difference would be wilful solitude
And taking to oneself the garden when
Mist, dark, and cold—oh, not to mention bye-laws—
Make it quite silly to be there at all.
(The critic asks, 'But where is it mysterious?')

You are alone now by the darkening waters,
Perhaps you ought not to be there at all.
The park's the same whatever you may say about it;
The nature of a thing may not be altered
By how we fiddle with linguistic structures—
Or may it not? For our awareness may be,
And our awareness postulates the nature,
And yet the nature always is itself,
And our awareness also is a part of
The larger nature we would postulate
Even a god to be aware of once.
(The critic says, 'But where is it mysterious?')

Or have you ever travelled in the tube
Jogging and tired, and watched these other glances
As tired and as inquisitive as yours?
Is there a brooding mind of groups and places
Or has the body its transparencies?
The mind a place, about the eyes and mouth,
About the relaxed hands and jogging knees,
Of self-expression, and a place behind
The noble forehead to be safe in hiding?
But is it hidden, is it ever safe?
Think, its adventure and its safety too
May be in this publicity of knowing.

Where there's no mist, perhaps most mystery:
I have pondered long on these things till I feel
(Though I am tired now and I say this slackly)
That when the pressures heap up all together
And we've this sense of knowing what we never
Could say—this sense, 'There's something, and I feel it'—
(The honest child will ask you: 'Where's the something?
I see the lamps, the curling mist, the trees.')
The park's then altered by our way of seeing:
'And the eye altering,' Blake said, 'alters all''
It is not just a muddle about language,
A tension or fatigue that we project.

It is, though it has no precise location;
It is a something that our words are for.
There are more ways of knowing than we know of
Somehow we know the ways we do not know.

That is the thing. The poetry is not elsewhere,
It is the mist, the faces in the carriage,
It is that now the days are drawing in,
Or that when you are talking to another
You know by more than words and more than gestures,
More than the mind and eye take in, a being.
It is the rain in trochees on the tarmac,
The rosebush bending in the autumn wind.
It is the lamplight on the evening river,
Red, shaking, as the cosy bus goes by.
Or all the glittering domes and spires of London,
Majestic in the cold, from Waterloo,
And, near, the smoke, the crowds, the hooting trains,
The smell of bitter in the public bar,
The lapse of care, the spread of conversation
Through a long afternoon in opening rings,
It is how odd we should be here at all,
And here should be. It is the privilege
And the excitement of our conscious being
In such a context; when, the clock forgotten,
And the untimely distance of the stars,
We have the sense of a perennial solace
And a majestic state, though fallen, or though
A state that altering alteration finds.

We have the sense that patient clouds are passing,
That there's one hue, one flavour, swaying shadows
Cast by one plane-tree on the windy road.
Full glasses on the bench upon the pavement,
And the gulls wheeling by the swollen river
For scraps, the long tugs chugging up and down.
In mere abstraction we can turn in terror
From all the life about us, but we love it
Too with a love more deep than hate or fear.
It is high adventure to be human,
Young man. You mourn for this unlucky age.
If I were young like you and were a poet
Though I should grieve there would be joy beneath it.
Is there not also joy beneath your grief?
The joy and grief of one linked various process,
One fountain, one great horn of plenty which
Also sparse cunning, also Chinese vases
Rounded from thinnest clay, transforming light
To commentaries upon the mind's precision,
Also a Turner picture, say a late one,
Some blobs of pink, some yellow, some blank canvas—

A cliff, a castle, and a field with cows—
Or new chaste patterns of squares and circles,
Also these praise. A poet is a praiser,
A maker and a shaper. Make and shape,
Young man, your monument to all this grasping.
It is your being that I shape and praise.

For Tilly, Sick, with Love

People don't give such parties now. The young men are old.
You would curl on the carpet. Your thin pretty fingers unrolled,
Pulling pins out, your coils. They came down, a straight weir of green gold...

People don't give such parties now. The young men are old,
Busy with social do-gooding or class self-importance:
More on the make than we were, if all were told.

So little we had, and so gay, it is something to ponder:
Fringes and dirndls; guts twisted by weak, wersh beer,
Salami, Algerian wine-cup, hard cider, and spam.

And the talk going on till the man in the flat downstairs
(Who knew you at Oxford) comes up with his baby and swears
And out to the hot smoky London night we scram.

It rolled down your waist, little mermaid. The clever young men
Would leave their tall talk about Sartre, and come to you then,
As I came, old precious, as never I did not come—

I know what Time brings: I dance slow, to a Noh-play drum!—

All a-goggle. Oh what, the young men would say, could you be,
With your sweet puppy face, light blue eyes that seemed hardly to see,
Long sweet legs, a child's body? Oh, Goddess of Liberty,

You seemed all men's and no man's. Sweet child, in the mist of your stare
I am lost (you lie ill now) in love and not in despair:
I am lost in the green-gold cascade of your merciful hair

Drowning the knowledge, more deep, of how deep now your pain.
I would put out my hand in the dark to hold your hand.
I would bear your pain, if I could, in the waking night.

All I can say, sweet, is perhaps not just this land
Makes and destroys the image of delight.
Had a gay Muse ever so pure a brow?
God considers conditions. We shall meet for a drink again.
Is our love round you? People don't give such parties now.

The Insane Philosophers

And tense under a front-row desk the legs,
Flattered by shadow, of a promising
Second year female held his philosophic
Attention gripped: 'Sir, may I have my essay
That says that everything is fluctuation?'
'Your legs at least...your legs are real,' he said.
She said, 'They change with the eternal flow,
And with your mood, philosopher, in the evening.'
He said, 'Are real and also beautiful.'
She said, 'To you, and at a certain distance.'
He said, 'To stroke them would be real and good.'
She said, 'It would to you, and not to me.'

She seemed to be an exemplar of his theme
But vanished into relativity,
Leaving him, massive and confused, alone,
A stolid man, with stolid contemplations:
His grossness and his distance from the real.
He thought: 'Our Mother is Reality.
I have forgotten what our Mother looks like
And may not now return towards that shore
Where the Unborn sport beside our sea.'

In came his new assistant, sinister,
Came Dr Arid, with the clacking hands,
Who cack-cawed: 'We can talk about the girl.
I think the things we say of her have meaning.
If cheap and acrid smells still stain the air,
Or if I think of bluebells and new hay,
Or of the sun and of the smell of seaweed,
My senses will confirm she was with you.
In worn emotive words, she was a Muse.
It is true but trite to say she was a girl.
That does not give us any information!'

His elder sighed: 'How real and beautiful!'
'Blobbo, you should be a poet,' Arid replied.
'Your world of notions is unreal to me:
I half believe in what I might have touched.'

'And in love, Arid?' Blobbo gurgled and gooped.
'In a force moving through us, forward and back,
In the great dance, in the hands holding the strings?

The joints of that wooden puppet went all slack;
Arid, discrete limbs on the class-room floor!
Blobbo went to a party and drank too much,
Came back home, slept, explored the floors of sleep,
Where one drowned man is all philosophers,
And listened to a dialogue in himself:
His idealist said: 'I want to eat my mother':
His realist said, 'My Mother to eat me!'
Into the dream came clacking Arid again:
'You are together and are a single man,
Your Mother will not eat you or be eaten!'

The sleep went deeper, silvered up again,
He saw the great sea stretching out for ever
Under a silver sky without a sun;
He saw the dotted dolphins loping homewards,
And each one had a poet on its back;
He smelt the class-room smell of chalk and ink-wells,
Drunkenly blessed the Whole, and sunk in darkness,
But through the darkness knew the great sky also
And heard the children laughing on the shore.

Lenten Meditation

It is hard to forgive, ever, even the dead:
My father who put on an act which was not himself
But which he imposed on me: my mother who talked:
Whose talk gnawed into my thinking and self-being:
My sister whose strength was a reproach to my weakness:
The louts at school and college who struck or mocked me:
The war, the roaring sergeants, the wool-brained officers:
The drunken bohemians with half my brains who insulted me:
The women who refused my love, and the women who accepted it:
The fools and rogues whose boots I had to lick
To earn a pittance: the possible young poets
Who ate my heart and spat away the gristle:
The Great Master, a bibulous charlatan:
The White Goddess, in the end a blowsy whore:
The Teachers, vain, tetchy, malicious pedants:
The Old Chums, pilfering one's books and bottles
And chumbling one's fame to death over their cups:
It is easier, much easier, to wish them dead
And to wish eternal fire to avenge one's injuries.

One could have lived on water and bread in an attic.
Like barracudas they ripped up one's life. And one had
To produce love for all those who devoured one.
That is the point of Lent.

The spring blossoms,
Like little nobbles of hellfire pumped through a tree,
One cannot help loving them: cats, children, sunsets,
The blue through diffused clouds, such small bribes!

How often, how often, how often, how often, I
Might have destroyed it all by a single wish:
The deep dark, and no more cheating of light!
But that I suppose is the whole meaning of Lent.
Wine becomes vinegar. Comradeship sacrifice.
Sleep a sly treachery. Waking extreme pain.

God comes down to pay more than our price.
Let us hold on. No doubt He will waken again.

For William Empson's Fiftieth Birthday

The enormous room is crowded, the wine is red:
The extraordinary luminous eyes in the backcast head
Of this institution, epithet, joke, sage
As famous as Pepsodent or Basic English
Confront their own world over our heads with a tinglish
Coiling shock. He is an electric eel
From whom our soft flat flounder thoughts rebound:
He stirs up in his own air his own sea
Of lithe prehensile ambiguity
Where in the deeper waters the light changes
Over sunk words like hidden mountain ranges
To what, to our eyes, seems opacity:
But his fanbeard of a Japanese luckgod reaches
Out of that sea to proliferate on our beaches
In a popping tangle of fruitful misapprehension:
'Oh, to be sure, to be sure! Now that you mention...'
The mind is a vortex, thoughts have their own round
In a wilder and wittier than Highland reel,
Splutter and flutter with a Bengal match's rage.

He taught us thinking is a kind of feel
And how to read, and wonderfully misread, a page!
But who has plumbed the poet's narrow sound?

Autumnal Elegy

It is another autumn, the air closes
Around the large low moon with a blue constriction,
Round the reluctant leaf with a crisping hand.
The little winds make wispy crepitation.
The easy heat and rage are gone, the bland
Debility of summer. One supposes,
Poised on the downward slope of hesitation,
The thunder and the sweat were both a fiction:
Though housefronts shone with paint and shops with roses.

Around the large low moon with a blue constriction
The poet pulls his scarf of commonplaces,
Of luckless love and chilly assignation,
Too wrapped in thought against the cold to care
Though native woodnotes spiral to inflation
Or how her light is dimmed by his depiction
Of that one eye with its albino glare.
For all the phrases are like old friends' faces
As dull as a no-more-explored addiction.

The poet pulls his scarf of commonplaces
Around his chilly fate. All art is hollow;
These are the words that moved us long ago
And now like smiles through smoke in public-houses
Can reassure us of a warmth we know.
We seek the moment where it left its traces.
Some cry, beneath the moon's mask sleeping, rouses
The hounds to bay again, the hunt to follow,
And Actaeon to show his ghostly paces.

Around his chilly fate, all art is hollow
Like the long street with intermittences
Of light, such eyes, upon its dark façades.
The dogs are round him in the empty air.
This is the truth imagination adds
To smoke, to chatter, to the beer we swallow,
To conversations broken on the stair.
Our death is fed to us in magic pittances:
And these blank walls are faces of Apollo.

Like the long street with intermittences
Of light, our life. These autumn evenings move us
With beckoning windows, like the lamps of port:
The lives of others, that seem safe and warm,
As our lives seem to their lives, by report.

If exiled souls could live on these remittances
From other exiles, and sleep out the storm,
The heavens might rumble but could not reprove us:
No debt would ever meet its day of quittances.

Of light, our life, these autumn evenings move us
To make some shining show, to help the others
Who move with trepidation through the dark,
Who lost the hope of harbour long ago,
And only hear the hounds of Actaeon bark.
But are there Watchers still who hate and love us,
Is there one Light by which all lights burn low?
Or only wanderers like ourselves, our brothers?
O Glow, O Guide, enlighten and approve us!

To make some shining show, to help the others,
May be one more of our deciduous poses
Heaped in its corner by the tidy year
And rising now in aromatic sorrow.
We fear, and we have reason for our fear,
Since hope lies gasping and the fire smell smothers
All we can guess of perfumes of tomorrow,
Smoke of the tripod tickling our noses,
We wonder now if any Sybil bothers.

Maybe one more of our deciduous poses
Will spike with green the sullen avenue
And beak the buds to cry at desperation
The brief defiance of another spring.
Though souls are not a vegetable nation
But more like rocks that need a second Moses,
To these recurrent images they cling.
The year is spent, and we have spent our revenue.
It is another autumn, the bank closes.

A Letter Full of Hate

A letter full of hate. Hate answers back.
One burns the letter, burns one's reply.
Feels like a bad man on a quite good rack.
Keeps on composing answers. Wonders why.

One should forgive all injuries, of course.
And one had swallowed many insults, too.
To shout against the wind would make one hoarse.
To spit against the wind, uncleanly, too.

Poor, without talent, ugly, envious, vain,
Listed to think himself a saint and bard,
Lopsided pillar in the winds of pain,
Whom nature, luck, and not one's own luck marred,

And yet one's own luck (if he knew it all!)
Stands as his symbol of foul compromise
With papers, pennies, people at its call,
So heaven forgive one, yes...but damn one's eyes!

And one's first rancour, gathering weight from his,
Heaves up the phrases that would smash him flat;
Becomes his gibbering antithesis
And then recoils, in stammering fear, from that,

So many devils from a small scrawled page!
So much do opposites communicate!
One crawls in terror from the sprawl of rage,
The bloody spill of all the soul in hate!

Some habit of indifferent good will,
Not tenderness or lust, is proper love.
Well only numbly not to wish him ill
Wrestle! And, rigorous, patient powers above,

Who shape one to ironic purposes
And buy one's acquiescence with the sun,
Teach one to see the truth in what he says:
Perhaps he is a better man than one.

The Decade

With all the detail easy to forget
And like the feeling of an empty room
That smells a little bit of murder yet,

Pray for a world that labours in the womb
And for your own past promise that you met
Transfixed to this decade, as to a doom
That smells a little of an empty room,

Or of a wall, where, peeling in the wet
Night, the loud posters blue away to gloom
With all the detail easy to forget

And such lost faces through the darkest loom,
Lacking love's comfort, that for ever fret...
That smells a little, of an empty room,

Gone, and for other guests the tables set
Who now aspire the city to assume
That smells a little bit of murder, yet

Where searching for a seer, we strike on whom?
The singer of a day, his song to let,
Transfixed, to this decade, as to a doom!

Ours the gapped sites of lives, and ours to let:
These weeds, this rubble, offer—oh, to whom,
With all the detail easy? To forget

Now all the wizardry the weak assume,
The formal tasks by false ambition set,
That smells a little of an empty room,

Shadows and shadows, where our memories fret
And weave their cloth of nothing on a loom
That smells, a little bit of murder yet

Most certainly my nights recall, a gloom
Where paper poems foundered in the wet,
Transfixed, to this decade as to a doom

Part of my life. It was the part I met
Transfixed to this decade as to a doom
(Withal, the detail easy to forget)
That smells a little bit of murder yet,

Transfixed to this decade, as to a doom
With all the detail! Easy to forget,
That smells a little of an empty room.

Yin and Yang: A Dialogue

He: So fingers shape, so heat bakes clay
That it becomes unearthly stuff,
Drinking the amber of the day
And sure it cannot hold enough.

She: I swirl with day like glassy gold,
Like straw-transparent Nippon tea:
How thin my cup, what fire I hold,
What luminous liquidity!

He: A moment when the wave is high
And like a Hokusai dragon curled,
A moment when we love and die
Your thin glazed substance props the world!

She: I am no cup, I am your shore,
My grains worn fine beneath your wave.
My shape is what is yours no more,
I thrust between you and the grave.

He: Like water in a cup, my sea
Is held within your cup of lands.
Only the shape you take is me
And I am water in your hands.

She: But not to close the trope too soon
Or press the metaphor too much,
Some other, distant as the Moon,
Controls the tides she does not touch!

He: But not to let the theme run on
Or lose the chance to point a moral,
Am I not your Endymion?
And with yourself why should you quarrel?

She: No, Earth, not Moon, my shores must suffer
Breakers of alien unrest:
Mere moonshine moves you to me, constant lover:
Child, ocean, landlocked in my laughing breast!

Brockham End House

(for George and Olga Lawrence)

'Lawrence, of virtuous father, virtuous son...'
Putative ancestor! The proved one's bust
Stands in your hall, a long, grave, bony face
That suits with marble. 'Here lies Henry Lawrence
Who tried to do his duty.' In the long
Unlighted corridor I explore your books,
'Lawrence and Havelock: Heroic Lives.'
Dust gathers here on Sleeman and on Meadows
And on 'The Chronicles of Dustypore'.
Here, on a shelf, an Empire's rise and fall,
And half an hour here from the bus to Bath
The little hills that 'run into your face'
Enclose a steep demesne of woods and pasture
Where the forget-me-not among the nettles,
The tame white rabbit chasing Chinese geese,
The low clouds gathering on the view of Bristol,
The fair and feathery pencilling of tall trees,
Bluebells, primroses, very early cowslips,
Mare's-tails, molehills like stepping-stones in grass,

Moss on the dry-stone dykes, all work together
With the sheep's morning meh, the rooks' cawing,
An unidentified bird on a cherry tree
That sounds like a baby's rattle, strawberries,
Giant strawberry plants, that are to climb up canes,
And fennel rooted up to cook with fish,
Your cider from the cask, your English beef,
Your friend the Everest climber, who throws up
A new-laid egg to prove it will not break
Upon the lawn, and breaks three eggs in turn,
All work together, as I say, to make
Me, a townee, sink back in generations
To when my folk were farmers in Caithness:
Most bleak to this, but the land's feel remains:
London seems far in purgatorial smoke
And it seems heaven up on your high ridge.

Two Poems

I

Time, left to stand, grows sour within the jar.
Time, spilling, leaves its stain upon the floor.
So only moving keeps us where we are.

What has the traveller got from coming far?
The young know less and they imagine more.
Time, left to stand, grows sour within the jar.

In the far city the familiar bar
Turns the raw poet to the musty bore.
So only moving keeps us where we are.

What words preserve, brooding on words will mar.
Do not avoid the traffic and its roar.
Time, left to stand, grows sour within the jar.

Mind is the driver and the world its car;
We only rise if everything can soar,
So only moving keeps us where we are.

Our stocks in time are never quite at par,
We never enter any final door.
Time, left to stand, grows sour within the jar;
So only moving keeps us where we are.

II

That gap of grief, now fruitless to explore —
The aching hollow in experience —
It could not help, or hurt or harry more.

Some dig like moles, and some like eagles soar;
Most pat its crust with feeble paws of sense,
That gap of grief now, fruitless, to explore.

If nothing's there, there's nothing to deplore;
No case for frankness or for reticence.
It could not help or hurt or harry more.

I feel strong waves about my sullen shore
And wish that they might beat more black and dense
That gap of grief, now fruitless, to explore:
It could not help or hurt or harry, more.

A Variation on Wordsworth

Thoughts that do often lie:
    too deep for tears
Or vain excuses, lady, of any sort,
Thoughts that do often tear too deep for lies
Too often rasping at my heart resort.

It is the metaphysical scullion mind
Below the accepted failures and forgiven sins
That might, perhaps, induce these lying tears,
Peeling off attitudes like onion skins:
They only are the smarting of sore eyes.
It is the swaggering master above stairs
Outswears disaster with his tearing lies,
By his eyes' blaze his brilliant doom defined.

Or, indeed, at some abject depth the true tears lie,
In the child that is wild with bellowing rage, being born —
Later by a long tide
His slack skin thrust aside
To a shore where the wave curled
Of the open and wide
Moderately various world
Stings no more with its spray.
To wait for that wave is the war in the peace of our day,
But we find the round of a maze where we looked for rest
And strain, to the want of a wave, the swimmer's breast
And the posed soldier heart to the want of strife.
There is not enough life in our life:

Bricks, books, beer, routine,
And repeating what we mean
Till that becomes habit too.
When shall we know what we always knew?
The child cries, having shattered its glass shell,
The round innocent egg of unconscious being.
The man sulks silent, has built up too well
A cell around his seeing.

And yet one shall weep, lady, and know why:
The common crying of our lying kind,
Lurking like lions sulky in their sour lairs:
We all too much presume on our despairs
And each would be the Hamlet in this play.
To me the meanest skirt that blows can give
(Whipping around slim legs on a spring day)

Thoughts that are much too practical for verse
And foolish hopes, that keep me struggling on:
Cast me as Rosencrantz, I'll still rehearse.
Where shall I be, though, in a later time
With all these gentle titillations gone?
These small snatched pleasures build no lofty rhyme,
And crumble not the outer walls of fate:
We have a date with destiny, no doubt,
But miss our destiny to keep a date,
A small date, with the womb that shut us out.

Yet small constructions out of crumbling years
Mean something; yet your skirt against your thighs
Blown, your hand that sought mine in the taxi,
And yet the wanton welcome in your eyes!
Though Fate no doubt is waiting with his axe, I
Cannot regret all this. Though Time has spies,
Such shallow thoughts induce my facile tears:
Weep for the love that fears beneath our lies,
Weep for the lie that loves beneath our fears!

Other Poems of the 1960s

Instead of an Elegy [11]

Bullets blot out the Life-time smile,
Apollo of the picture-page,
Blunt-faced young lion
      Caught by vile
Death in an everlasting cage:

And, no more young men in the world,
The old men troop to honour him.
The drums beat glum,
      Slight snow is swirled
In dazzling sun, pale requiem.

And pale dark-veiled Persephone,
A golden child in either hand,
Stands by white pillars;
      Silently,
It seems she might forever stand.

In bright grey sun, processionals
Of pomp and honour, and of grief,
Crown that dead head
      With coronals.
Some stony hearts feel some relief:

But not your heart, America,
Beating so slow and sure and strong,
Stricken in his
      Triumphal car,
Guard Caesar's bitter laurels long

With solders' music, rites of war:
He had proved bravely when put on:
The soldiers shoot.
      Rage echoes far
Above the grave at Arlington.

How the Heart grows Cold [12]

Can I deny my love
Whose beauty was a fable?

It was my wish the weather
Would ever stay her colour.

And crystal was her winter.
Can I deny my love?

Whose autumn was a fable.
Of toasted leaves of story;
Whose winter heard the centaur
Crunch the eager snow;

Whose winter stood suspended
As from a frozen skyline;
Whose gesture was a window;

Whose summer a river
Of a late summer,
With the leaves soon falling;

Whose dear spring broke my heart
Against her green ice?

Was it on the seashore
Now or at another
Most unlucky season

Or where a fat blackbird
Under the sensuous shadow
Of glossy rhododendrons
Pecked the grass for worms?

Or was it by a river,
Turning for a parting
Casual and for ever?

But what a chilling light
From what angle falling,

Told the heart, *you burn*
With your own burning

And with the fire's dying,
The heart grows cold?

PART 2

Craving sun, or love, or water,
all I can offer you now is sleep.

Sleep is the last. The poets speak
of a fulness of our being,

I desire an emptiness
and to be empty of desire,

never more my fingers to play with
cigarettes or twirl the wineglass,

never more to hear your voices
raised so shrill, my birds, above

all the clatter of the winehouse:
I desire anonymous

less than a shadow to slip through
the gross holes, God, of your net

as the tiny fishes slip
or the contingent intentions or

the lucky chances that are not luck:
into a darkness like the thighs

into a deeper darkness, like
the shadows upon standing water

into the darkness of my speaking
into a sleeping with no pain.

Student Resurgence: A Verse Exercise

(Nine-syllable syllabics, all lines enjambed)

Something is happening in the
world at last, a sort of violent
thaw. I think of the grey hairs of my
worried colleagues (my own also) as
chunks of scurrying away, melting
drab grey ice. Ourselves and history
frozen so long, in a cocktail's tinkling
frigidaire cube, sweat down messily

into a turbid, a protesting
drainlike gurgle. Daddy or uncle
no longer knows or is supposed to
best, even in a wheezy clubman's
winking, boozy, and know-the-scorish
old chap way. Charles Dix, Metternich
pack their bags, Napoleon the Little
collapses in shoddy. Palmerston
munches five meat courses, a large slice
of very hard ham, last barrier
against God and Gladstone, perishes
to launch a 'New Age'.

    That 'New Age' was
flashy characters: Chamberlain Dilke
Gambetta Boulanger. No age-drop
ever brings truly in the rule of
saints or an unbogus bonanza.
New arrivals look over their shoulders
for hints of a lost style. History
becomes like a virus itch. Swinburne
curses both Boers and Buonapartes
and bliss is it in that dawn or just
usual false dawn? Let the mugwumpish
fuddy-duddies, the fat classical
liberals at least get a grin of
recognition on their creaking jaws
that it has happened, has all been said
before... Yes, but if it is just a
carrousel, the same wooden horses
coming round with a false surprise once
and once and once and once and again
why stop the machine? It is fresh to
children. History is at least a
great afternoon out, the garish fair
once more. Life is a bazaar and a
trap. Let life have anyway now its
fling. Proper indeed that these bushy
young Desmoulins pluck their leaf cockades
And stammer green vulnerable spring.

Tavern Muse

O Muse of many reckonings,
O tavern Muse, that gauzy night
If a compunction shook my heart
It also trembled with delight,

Muse, of man's life a thing apart
(Though others say that there should be
Full many a one of me for you
And only one of you for me):

O, half embodied in the blue
Of gauzy mist and spangled air,
Unweighted with incumbent hours
And bright with Berenice's hair,

Lady, you haunt phantasmal bowers
And sky in what disguise you choose:
Like Garbo in a rainproof now
And long slim feet in long flat shoes,

Next, Queen Christina at the prow,
Pride launching into Emptiness:
Or be a Muse of flesh and blood:
A shirr of silk, a whispering yes!

Or be (Desire) at drowning flood,
But then be faint, and far away.
The spangling air! The gauzy night!
But waving trees at wink of day,

White walls asplash with greenshot light,
Illusions of the cocktail bar!
Remind us, then, Persephone,
Remind us now, of what we are,

And tell us what we soon shall be
Pillowed beside you in drugged sleep.
Eurydice dissolved away.
O Muse of darkness, did you weep?

And, Orpheus alone in day,
Wife, mother, and the maiden (one)
Became a crowd to rend him limbmeal:
O Muse of reckonings, was it fun?

Sketches of Travel

I

TRAQUAIR

Dryden's broad face,
Lean Nithsdale.
The Bear Gates locked
Since the year of Culloden.

A house long lived in:
In the chapel
A charabanc tripper:
'What's a' this, Meg!
Episcopelian?'
'It's waur, Jemmy:
It's Papish!'

And NO POPERY scrawled
In big chalk letters
On a wall near
The charabanc depot.

And back in Pitlochry
The tweed-skirted ladies,
In the good little hotel
With the Japanese garden,
Shaking their heads:
'Thon Bernadette,
She needs a skelping!'

The old banners
Are still flying:
The old swords
Not unsheathed.

2

THE KYMMIN (MONMOUTH)

Park the car
Walk a little:
A Japanese temple
With wooden pillars
Curling roof top,
Rough stone foundation:
On medallions names
Of English Admirals.

The wooden walls came
From the Forest of Dean.
The simple worship
Of tribal heroes
Deified even
In their lifetimes.

And then the view
Down on Monmouth,
Neat confluence of
Monnow and Wye,
Tiny bridges,
Houses and people:
Aerial perspective
As in an
Eighteenth-century map.

All washed in the blue and clean
Summery Italianate air.

Memories of Swansea

Like the Bay of Naples, Landor said. I remember
Beer at the Mumbles, a little railway, gone now:
And to your right along the coast the dragonish
Sea-gobbling rocks, and Vernon Watkins's neighbour's
Greenhouse on the cliff that a sea-wind had come into
And broken like a too large hand in a too small glove.
That also had a twisted dragonish look.
We ate tomatoes plucked green from the tomato
Plants in the greenhouse, with that fruity dust
And pungent prickly smell of the freshly plucked.
Vernon said that the whole Gower Peninsula
Was a Saesneg enclave (Watkins is a little Wat).
A windy day. On the cliff, my children, small then,
Were swung off their feet between our hands.
A steep path down to the sea. My wife undressed
Under a rock shelter, in the slapping wind,
With Gwen, who said: 'If after you are forty
You give up this sort of thing, you *do* give up!'
The boiling boisterous slaphappy sea!
Vernon at ease on a surfboard. I sometimes
Floated over the rise of the big waves,
More often they bounced me gasping back. My son
Climbed a high rock and he could not get down.
I could not get up. Vernon swam up the surface,
As if rock were water, all casual muscle and nerve:
How right he should go in the sweat of a set of tennis!
We had tea later. Looked out of the window at
The play of light on clouds and birds and rocks,
The endless iteration, endlessly different —
A sort of metaphor for God in Nature —
Shape, colour, spray, all changing and unchanging,

He had become a bank clerk in Swansea to stare at
All his life, making slow poems of praise:
But I thought also, a long bus journey
For Gwen to go and do her shopping in Swansea
And rocks are not as talkative as neighbours.

I can still see his litheness, active on rock and surf:
And his beautiful horse-like asymmetrical face.
Much later at Leicester, at our Arts Festival,
His saying with Empson in the audience,
How Dylan's little smack or swoop at Empson,
That tiny parody intended to go into
John Davenport's spoof teccy (dear drunk, dead now!)
Was on the whole a joke rather than a tribute.
Blessed are those who bless a moment of memory.
Bless Kingsley Amis, also, since he lent me his
Terrace house with a greenhouse that had green
Just edible grapes, near Cwmdonkin Park.
Harold Frankel organised our Arts Festival,
Adored Vernon. This year I revisited Swansea
To visit Harold in the Morriston Hospital,
A fat man down to nine stone, a mature student
Of fifty-eight, with a tube in his oesophagus;
Bouncing in bed, scattering press cuttings,
A dying man, still crazy about poetry,
The nurses kind to his untidy ways.
Bless the peculiar openness, the utter
Surprising openness to the receptive stranger
Of fiery, tetchy, hospitable Wales...

Harold died in another month or two
In Oxfordshire, in a private adult
Educational College, Braziers, run by
Marianne Faithfull's father. Kingsley became
A public image, now I never see him:
But strangely, Braziers, Horace-Walpole Gothick,
Sheep nibbling right up to the ha-ha,
Is where Ian Fleming was born. In the library,
His nursery once, I thought of Kingsley and Harold
And of Swansea, and Vernon Watkins. A funny world.

I slam on all this loose associational gossip:
I ought to have done some research on Dylan Thomas:
I had a look at the terrace house of his childhood:
I found no hunchback in Cwmdonkin Park.

Memory, Landor said, is the Mother of the Muses
But not a Muse herself. These memories move me.
Gossip becomes a tired man's poetry.
Swansea and Naples. Mabon will understand.

Note: Mabon, a Welsh literary magazine, edited by Alun Jones at Bangor.

Poems of the 1970s

The Poem

In one's late years
it is like making love in one's late years:
one sprang too alert and eager once at the touch of
almost any hands, the swimming, swooning look of
any dark or blue eyes, the harsh or
mellow or shrill note
of many a woman's voice, the petting
after the party with the cheap wines:
how often the walk at night down to Battersea Bridge,
the weeping Indian girl (or she might be English,
and laughing), the easy embraces
waiting for buses on the King's Road.

The *a deux* lunches, the visits to Art exhibitions,
the week-end walks in the country with heartier girls,
ending so often in a sort of amorousness:
'Is this how you always spend Thursday afternoons?'

Older and older, and I am a teacher,
and every young girl is my daughter,
and I have a very strict professional code.
And I have seen through my own excitements.

For Katie on her Eighteenth Birthday

O little daughter of delight
And grave and lovely growing girl
Year after year you see the white
Snow flurry and pink blossoms swirl,
Year after year spontaneous joy
Drives you to pick up brush and pen,
Paint and translate and make a toy
Of what is labour to most men.

Spontaneously you make things grow
Out of your fingers and your eyes,
For what you feel you also know,
And what you see you realise
In growing art in shape or word
Or colour or a story told.
And yet you laugh, it is absurd
You think, it is all fairy gold.
And sometimes sorrow clouds your eyes
And anger for man's suffering lot
And noble indignations rise
Harsh from your heart, and sharply hot.
But always still the white snow swirls,
And always still the blossoms flurry,
And you, the dearest of all girls,
May take your time and need not hurry.

A Lesson in Humanity for the Children, out of Aristotle's 'Poetics' [13]

'Pity is aroused by
Unmerited misfortune,
Fear by the misfortune of
A man like ourselves.'

Learn to feel fear, children,
Even if you cannot learn
To feel pity: post-Christian pity
Is more than Aristotelian,
It is pity for
Merited misfortune.

Try out the lingo.
Let yourselves go.
Say, *Cat, Prod:*
Mick, Jock, Taffy:
Remember Prince Charlie
(on first donning the kilt)
'Now I would be a true Highlander
If only I had the itch!'
Taffy was a Welshman, Taffy was —
A what, an Inspector of Schools!
'How odd of God to choose
The' — *whos?*
Aberdeen an' twal' mile roun
And then whaur are ye?'
Lowland piety: 'To root out
Their Erse language and
Papish religion!'

Robert Graves quoting
A Midland *mot* on the Scots
In the First World War:
'They skite too much
And run too fast—
Both ways!'
(Towards the enemy
And away from him.)
We have a lot of tribal hatred
Going in ourselves
Even if there were no immigrants.
(And we are a bloody mixture.)

Say over a litany. *Krauts*
Eyties. Ice-creamers. Wogs. Wops.
Dagos. Frogs. Abos. Kaffirs.
Going back and back in time.
Paynim. Heathen. Picts. Mahound.
Bohunks. Huns. Yids. Spades.
Blackies. Nigras. Nips.
Chinks. 'When I am living
In the Midlands they
Are sodden and unkind.'
'Toffy-nosed bastards'
'Pseuds.' 'Gnomes.' 'Smarties.'
'A *Dutch* treat.' 'An *Italianate*
Englishman, the Devil
Incarnate.' '*Frenchified* kickshaws.'
'The *Pope,* meagre soup, and wooden shoes.'
Way back in the Middle Ages—
'*Jack Straw and his meynie*
Whan that they would the Flemings slee!'
Border ballads:

> *I wad burn Carlisle Castle doon*
> > *And slochen it sae in Inglis bluid*
> *That never a man in Cumberland*
> > *Wad ken where Carlisle Castle stood.*

'Scratch a *Russian*
And you find a *Tartar.'*
Take it out of race and
Nation. Skinheads. Hippies.
Students. Teachers. Aggro and
Bovver-boots. 'Long-haired
Louts,' mods, rockers, *Black Books*
About education...

'Mostly fools,' Carlyle said

About the human race: certainly
They take where tribal
Emotion is concerned, a lot
Of educating. Carry on, you can
Carry on indefinitely. Last century
After the Great Hunger, the Great Famine,
Irish immigrants to America, to Scotland,
To England, found great notices
On factory doors saying: 'NO IRISH
NEED APPLY.' Take the snob side:
'Cultured Cockney, Thames valley
Twang!' 'Bottom drawer, my dear!'
Both sides. Three sides. Proles. Bosses. Liberals.
(I am a Liberal, it is a dirty word.)

We live in little tribes
Protecting our territory
And our pecking orders:
Class, place, food-habits,
Suburban or supra-suburban social habits—
'We keep ourselves to ourselves,' or
'We rather keep open house'...
Restricted or pedantic or snobbish verbal codes:
How many words in our heads,
Shillings in our pockets...?
We don't invite the bus-conductor home:
Is it because he is a *coloured prole*
Or because he is a *white nigger?*
Or because essentially
This is still a three-part society,
Captains, sergeants, privates:
Minds, wills, hands?
Can it ever be other?
Is the whole notion of *community*
A fatuous dream?

Colour is only an instance.
This, that I have described, is the
Violent human farce. Let us remember that
The Cat or the Prod,
The Sikh or the Pakistani,
The demonstrator or the
Cop
Bashed up
Should arouse fear in us
Because, after all, we can all
Interbreed,
All intercommunicate
(Black hand on white hand, sex at least one of
The crossers of the Great Barrier Reef:
Poetry another crosser):

173

We are one not many species.
That bashed up person there
Is *'a man like ourselves.'*

And if we don't see that,
See it, smell it, feel it,
What is going to happen
To this dear country?
The great royalist Clarendon
Looking back on Civil Wars
Wondered what madness had come over
'The best-natured people
In the world'—the great philosopher Santayana
Too rosily in the sunset of Empire
Said: 'Never has the world had
Such boyish or such kindly
Masters...' What is going
To happen? Misfortune, but not
Unmerited misfortune?

Shall we deserve then
Proper pity? Every night, children, say,
Saying your prayers, when you feel tribal hate:
A man like ourselves.

Home Thoughts on Ireland

1

Twenty-six years ago my honeymoon
In a small guest house at Killiney Bay.
Tea, soda-bread, whole lobsters, in a wooden
Shack on the beach. A party for us where
The men all stood and talked around the 'groceries',
The drinks upon the tables, and the women
Sat straight-backed round the room upon hard chairs.

And in the actual grocer's shop, we drank
Sherry or whiskey long past closing time,
Ducked from the window when the Garda passed
Our host then sang 'The Wild Colonial Boy'.
And I from memory quoted Yeats's version
Of Swift's great epitaph. Two kinds of culture
Met lovingly in warm incomprehension.
In Dublin, on a Friday, in a Protestant
Eighteenth-century house with many portraits
Of Grattan and his like, we ate roast beef,
But our two Catholic friends had each whole lobsters.
Good holiday. It gave us indigestion.
In England it was still the rationing time.

The boy who sang 'The Wild Colonial Boy'
I do remember asking him the time
(A British fidget about licensing hours):
'Ah, what is Time? Come throw away your watch!'

Perhaps I threw it, and Time has not moved.

2

Twice or three times at Sligo? I forget.
All the Yeats scholars, the Americans,
And thinking there was precious little room
On Innisfree for bean-rows or for cabins,
And Yeats's tower all tarted up for tourists
The second time, so that the great inscription,
     'And may these characters remain
     When all is ruin once again',
Was nonsense. Coole Park truly desolate,
The house a ruin, answered expectation.
And the first time I drove round Lissadell
The trees seemed blighted by some greyish fungus.
I saw the house next time. Cracking plaster,
Paintings that need restoring. Our proud guide,
Himself a Gore-Booth, said, 'Yes, Yeats stayed sometimes.
Not in the best guest room. He awoke my grandfather,
Saying, "Sir Jocelyn, to-night I have seen
A ghost I have not seen for thirteen years!"
"Willie," my grandfather said, "go to your bed!"'

How one admires the pride of ancestry...
We saw stuffed birds, partridges, ptarmigans,
A bear, I think a fierce snow Arctic bear,
Shot by a loyal servant, as it lumbered
Over the ice to maul his Gore-Booth master.
A Conan Doyle world, not a Yeats world, really.
And sawdust stuffing coming out of the bear's paws.

3

You can't help liking Ireland if you like Ireland.
The boyos have killed six women and a chaplain
With some infernal device, at a safe distance,
And have scuppered off Scot-free. One should be angry,
But, God, one's too old for a bloody ballet
Of categories (reverse Bradley!): one is much more
Like Maudling who thought Bernadette was his cross
Grand-daughter, who got into his 'plane and said:
'What a bloody country! Give me a large whiskey!'
They are all human. Even old slouching Paisley,
Mouching, slouching, with his chomping chops:
As a cub reporter on *The Aberdeen Press and Journal*
I used to pick up subliterate sermon notes
From shambling Wee Free Ministers. They were much like him.

A bloody country, but the ballad is still alive,
And the bogs are the opposite of blood-red, a coaxing green,
You'd choke and drown in. Someone said a friend of mine
'Rode backwards out of an Irish bog, on a pig's back.'
She was in fact a very charming woman.

5

I shall go to Sligo this August and lecture on
'The Influence of Yeats'. And if they shoot me,
Or blow me up, in the Town Hall, in mid-quotation,
It will be after all a nice last touch.
For an otherwise tepid *Times* obituary!

6

But O my love, and O the Irish shore!

A Performance of 'The Bacchae'

(by students on the hundredth anniversary of the first publication of Nietzsche's 'The Birth of Tragedy')

Plenty of horror and not pity. Dionysus
Is the hero, Phoebus, of light and order,
Mentioned with perfunctory courtesy just once.

In place of pity what N calls 'festal cruelty':
And against the horror the poetry of woven flowers.

E wrote this play in his old age, getting out of
War-shattered Athens to semi-barbarous
Macedonia. Swinburne went puke at
Euripides' 'warm-dropping of lyric tears':
I'd have thought this a pretty Swinburnian play,
Though E, disillusioned with being Socratic,
Finds something to puke at in the dark gods too.

I like poor Pentheus, honest Tory, male chauvinist,
Very suspicious of this new Black Power god
Leading women into the mountains to get up to
God knows what. Yet ironically it is the
Superficially gentle god of excess
Warns Pentheus to try to keep his temper...
Honour any god. You will not understand him.

'Festal cruelty' as farce, poor Pentheus
Babbling in drag, most indecently eager
To voyeurise mama busy at her mountain sex.
Cadmus and Tiresias, dotards, false dangling phalluses:
Creaking old limbs to climb on the Bacchic bandwagon!

Wood, leaf, bird song. Before they start tearing
Men and beasts to pieces, the wild women
Suckle gazelles or kids. Weave flowers for thyrsis.
A more than Moses, Bacchus by a thyrsus miracle
Springs from moor and rock wine, water, milk.

And then horror. Lovely, blood-spattered Agave
Home with the head of a young mountain lion,
Sobered up by a quite different Cadmus,
Gazing at the head of her son she has wrenched off.

Terribly topical, dearie, to be sure!
N and E were very much on our wave-length.
Aristotle was just an old boring instructor.
But Apollo is still a dangerous god at his distance!
His bright arrows, the unfaceable sun!

University Road Graveyard [14]

Across the road from the university buildings,
    Behind trees, gravestones stand
And forgotten respectable Edwardian citizens
    Possess this land.

There beneath the gritty grass sleep the prosperous
    Of a humdrum age,
Each with his name and date in large letters
    On a stone page.

There they laid to rest the small knitwear fortunes
    And the glacier mints;
On polished granite mixed light industry
    Glitters and glints.

And the young Turks in the Senior Common Room
    With each sip they sup
From a cup of coffee wait very eagerly
    To plough that up.

On the turf-covered crushed bones they hope to see arising
    New Attenborough Towers
And longer echoing chambers for the noise of their
    Own mortal hours.

Colleagues and Students ¹⁵

One is bored by victims less,
Hates fellow-torturers more
Except that for them as for one
The ending of more is less,
Less wishing for something more
Than being the talking one

To the listening and shut-off many
(With fifty minutes to go
And the first five and the last
Leave a middle thirty too many)
Before we rise and go
From what might be the very last

Time we had said all that
And they had taken their notes
That might afterwards make sense
If we *did* make sense of that,
Were in tune with our own notes
Or touched their wits with a sense

Of being the trumpet through which
A great dead man can sound
With a hound-in-cry's voice:
But not to torturers, which
Is why boredom and hate must sound
In an easy — at ease! — voice:

And why one will not thrive
Wishing them all alive
And must put out of one's head
Prayers that they drop dead
Before one can rise and go
Knowing some cared to know.

Two Epigrams

1

TWO WIVES, ONE HUSBAND

The first wife calls the next 'a whining trollop':
    I like both wives. It's him I'd like to wallop!

2

AN ACADEMIC ADMINISTRATOR

A colleague says: 'A bully and a lout!'
He has our jobs within his hands no doubt,
But how can we placate his power-lust fully?
'Bully for you, you honest hearty bully!
Since we shall not be in, if you are out,
Over your fences, Bully Bottom, lout!'
Since wine of hate sours down to vinegar,
Salute bold Bottom...as a 'character'!
Thus in academies do souls survive,
By sugaring hate to keep sour love alive:
And let this thought console you in the night:
The higher up, the further out of sight!

Two Logic Poems

1

'The present
King of France
is bald or
purple but
not both, or
bald or purp-
le or both
or neither.'

'No comment.
I have not
the honour
of having
met the Comte
de Paris!'

2

'We can't be
friends. Let's still
be lovers!'

Flash Harry

(for George Barker's sixtieth birthday)

Flash Harry I used to call that one,
The man for the three-card trick,
The thimble-rigger, the con-man
With a loverly golden prick,

The cap with perhaps a razor-skip,
The scarf, the moll called Elsie,
Holding hunched court in a Fulham pub
Not in my snobby Chelsea,

One for a 1930s movie,
LEGS DIAMOND RISES AND FALLS!
Does George write 'poems' or 'poetry'?
Nobody doubts he has balls!

Gorgeous gaudy verses
Of a Fairground Pearly King,
A Barker? (But role rehearses
Soul...soul is everything?)

Bully-boys can be kind,
In a Fleet Street pub George pled:
'You are grand on Yeats...I was rude...don't mind!'
'I rise with my subject,' I said.

Little I've seen of you since.
You have had Women and Fame.
Which cuts to tastier mince
As old teeth get tired of the Game?

Men imagine and find it true.
I imagined suburban peace
And loving students. And did you
Imagine Guilt and Release? —

For lately when I fixed you
To read here, Release felt bland.
You were raffish and cocky at sixty,
But oddly, informally grand.

Men envy and fear the know-how
Of the Fates they have not had:
But I think of your life with love now.
(It was I, not you, went mad...)

I wish you an autumn drink, O
Of a shining New England sort:
Verse silky as maple and gingko:
And love and luck, old sport!

1972

Two Letters from, and a Conversation with, a Poet

1

'Also because I wanted
To finish her book and to return it.
I have now finished it; or with it — for I have not
Read all of it, and have skipped a good deal even
Of the core. It's the kind of book it is easier
To write than to read.
She really writes very badly indeed — abstract.
Humourless, and out of any (to me)
Recognisable context. Perhaps that *is*
Her American side? But yet with the Jewish
Religious passion of a Simone Weil,
In a way,
I find it lovely and splendid that she
Should see the world in terms so deeply true
In intent. I can also see why she (as she says)
'Gave up' being a poet; because
She never was one,
And doesn't see the here and now, the
Minute particulars with the eye of an artist.

'And perhaps started on philosophy too late
To be more than
A certainly lovely curiosity. I feel her mind
Energizes in a void.'

The writer long loved:
The subject at a distance
Become a friend, lonely but not lonely,
Lovely I think (in the letter as in most letters,
n is almost exactly like *v*).
The writer loved whom I knew in her youthful beauty,
With her first fresh music singing in my ears:
But the subject keeping Atlantic polite distances
In her void, if it is a void, retaining dignity,
Compelling respectful compassion without exacting it,
The subject one reveres.

But the subject, from others, excites other attitudes:
'It is not her madness or her wicked malice I hate so much
As her inability to write decent English prose!'

2

A poet in my title means, I should explain, two poets
And different letters,

And the conversation is with a third,

But the topics, the nature of poets and character of poets
Intersect: as I was asked, here, for three poems
And have written three, but they may be read as one.

'X was remarkably wrong about Basil Bunting,
Who is a remarkable poet. The Fulcrum Press
Produced his *Collected Poems* very finely. Does
It still exist? I certainly find it difficult
To believe that the young really understand
The Cantos. Pound himself doesn't
To judge from the extraordinary meeting
I had with him in Rome a few years ago...'

(And the second poet is two poets! They are speaking
In a similar tone, saying the same sort of thing.)

'I'm afraid my mother's Scottish (by birth),
Prolixity comes out in me worse than yours
In you (more Scottish than the Scotch). I had to stop here
And I've rather lost
The thread of my dialogue (or monologue perhaps). I don't
Feel very hopeful for my future, because
(Apart from disagreeing with everybody in my uncontrite way),
All the influential people are quite new
And devoted to new-Oldness I see everywhere
Or they are my enemies in so far as...'

(But one mustn't use the personal parts of a letter!)

'The differences in my new poems
Which you hit on so accurately
Should be seen in this context. I always react
To the trends of the time, and if this reading
Of them is correct, then I think greater satire,
More savage (and direct) attacks are necessary,
Even at the risk of sometimes seeming
Merely splenetic and peevish. So too with
Being more personal and less indirect. I haven't
Taken this up as an overall criterion, but
I find one of the few things that are an
Improvement in the present climate a rather less

Inhibited atmosphere. It is easier
To be personal and direct without
Being pounced upon, and held up as a
Bad example — "Look, he is being
Personal and direct!" '

3

*Veronica in the Critical and Critical and Critical
Methodology and No Holds Barred Seminar:*

'Poetry is at once conventional and rational.
That skylark, that cuckoo, that nightingale.
All three poets knew the bird was not listening
And could not, and would not, answer back!

W. knew perfectly well it was
A physical bird and not a wandering voice.
S. knew it was a bird not a spirit and that whatever
Biological needs impelled its song
Had no affinity with human emotions.
K. knew that nightingales have a short life-span,
Short indeed, compared to the average human!
Shelley would rather re-read his excellent poem,
I suspect, than listen to skylarks all day long!
But that convention is like grammar, metre, rhythm,
All the devices for freshening a worn *topos*...
The birds are *birds in a poem,* they are not *birds*...

'Look: it is like: it is perfectly arbitrary
That the word 'cat' means cat. You all know that one.
No resemblance between the word and the creature.
But, on the other hand: 'cat' *must* mean cat,
This is a convention, rational and necessary,
If you are intending to talk the English language!
Language as a system is rational, though every item
Looks arbitrary or artificial in itself.
A poem is a small system, language a large one:
Convention, the arbitrary, the artificial
Work all the way down. "And how are you, Charles?"
One doesn't expect a detailed account of his symptoms.
Experience is not 'experience' until it has been
Verbalised in a convention. Poetry, amusingly,
Can set two conventions clashing:

> *O cuckoo, shall I call thee bird,*
> *Or but a wandering voice?*
> *State the alternative preferred*
> *With reasons for your choice.*

Two conventions, the afflatus of the Romantic ode,
The rigour of the Oxbridge exam question,
Set clashing. But the thing works because
By a lucky accident it is perfectly grammatical,
By a lucky accident perfectly rhymes and scans...'

V. goes on to castigate what could be called
'Ordinary language' poetry: for instance:

> *Shaving this morning, I looked out of the window.*

'A banal remark, so trivial in fact that
One can hardly even imagine the occasion
When it would be worth making in "ordinary life".'

I said: 'Veronica, I agree. But suppose that
We take *this morning* not as an adverbial qualifier
Of the transitive participle *shaving,* but rather
As its noun-object. The thought of the poet
Engaged in such an awesome, unimaginable task
As shaving the morning, and yet retaining the nonchalance
To look out of the window! A poetic thought!'

A prosy poem, this, about a new poetics:
But young poets are looking for a new poetics:
People write to me, people talk to me, insights come:

> *The soul's dark cottage, battered and decay'd,*
> *Lets in new light through chinks that Time has made.*

Make me an Offer

Make me an offer, only a few days
To go.
Then the mist and the snow.
This is our most brilliant autumn, in its final blaze.

All that I have to offer to Poetry
Is only a few days.

Clearance sale, at enormous loss!
I have noticed the polar swing of the weather cock.
I am practically giving away what I have in stock,
Solid old-fashioned metre that wears for years,
Tears, idle, but wonderfully durable tears,
Lines that go swig and go swog, like a rocking horse:
Seventeen sigh-heaving sonnets, all handmade,
For I used to cater for the carriage trade.

It is supermarket weather, we must not sigh.
Make me an offer for life even when I
Am clearing my little shop
And the wind stops blowing and the crisp leaves come to a stop
And the dead tree's hollow bole has a fungoid crop.

Make me an offer
Even if only of copper
Leaves of the autumn ending
Crinkly and ready for spending
There was also a rich sick summer and a sweet sour spring.
Autumn itself has metallic crackle and zing.
Winter will not be the end of everything.
Life is not wholly an instantly disposable thing.

Only a few days.
Shutting up shop, try to praise
The enriched ash, not the quick knife:
The autumnal smell of the compost-happy heap.
Some thoughts about sleep.
Praise life.

Buy it, buy it, buy it, or let me burn it:
Pain is not given out with the rations, you must earn it.
Make me an offer for pain.

Praise life for a heart and not a stone is breaking.
Think about waking.
Think about praise.

You may take over my shop and many days.
But wait for the spring rain.

A Napkin with Veronica's Face, not Christ's [16]

1

'Leaving us only woe, which, like the moss,
Having compassion of unburied bones,
Cleaves to mischance and unrepaired loss':

Leaving us woe to heap, as heavy stones
Humped to that high cairn's top of Knocknarea
Avert worse woe, if offered woe atones

For the blue gorgon glare of sudden sea,
Bright, swooping, savage, after bog, mud, mist
Have clogged our passion down to piety

185

For Maeve, the rockfast queen of falconed wrist,
Who lives in stories, and who never was,
And yet her quern can grind us down to grist,

Leaving us only awe and windlestraws:
Stark on her kestrel roost with rakehell claws,

2

Leaving us only woe which, wan as clouds
Brushing some nibbled round low Border hill,
Mists the sheeps' wispy backs in woolly shrouds

While high above the sea-bent birds are shrill
And move towards that blank wall of Tantallon
Whose blankness speaks us neither good nor ill

But says the rider of the horse is gone
Who rose this country since she was a girl
And Pegasus perhaps she rode upon

And heard haar pipers of the North Sea skirl
And while she twirled her rein with easy hand
Had all the thoughts in that wild head aswirl

Because debatable she found her land:
No soul could sing for heart to understand.

3

Swift years by weeping willows by the Cam
Fed mind to soul and added hurt to heart
And, to love's power to bless, its power to damn:

So that there seemed a mockery in her art,
Delight in sorrow, sorrow in delight,
And word from world set warningly apart

Reading no riddle with the answer right
Except that in the dark all cats are gray
And in the utter dark all grays are white

And when cats sleep the mice come out to play
And nibble at the corners of old books
And gnaw a lot of learned rind away:

But blur their eyes perhaps and blear their looks:
So that one broth is spoiled by many cooks.

4

A broth of learning seemed to blur her mind,
A rich aroma, and but one stir more,
One pinch of herb, and surely she would find

The great elixir and the hidden lore
To make her the immortal Harlequin
Of death-blue profile on Picasso's shore

And all her thoughts were angels on a pin
Or plunging horses on a carousel,
Whirling around, or weaving out and in,

Were webs of tapestry she knew so well
She'd stretch it wide to make the world her maze,
That mighty maze one word that she could spell

And cast a spell on, till the blinding ways
Of worlds, by words, she'd bind in nights and days.

5

Madness, illusions of omnipotence!
I am a poet, I have known them too.
You have outsoared the shadow of our sense,

I cannot check your flight, or soar with you:
Poor dead girl, choking on your messy pillow,
Poor plunging planet, to disaster true

As flowing water to the thirsty willow:
Shall any brine-wet word of yours remain,
Jetsam or flotsam, tossed upon the billow

Of gaping Time, or of my useless pain
Wooing your ghost's grace with this artifice?
'In evening dress on rafts upon the main'.

Style is the answer: it comes down to this.
Whirl to the wings, young dancer. Blow a kiss,

6

For 'unsubstantial death is amorous'
And of our ghostly audience last to leave.
I saw you whirl so. I would hold you thus,

Tense teasing harlequin, and would not grieve:
Fierce innocent, you died and felt no shame,
Only loss, love, the ardour to achieve

(High spirit, blooded by the spur of Fame!)
The laurel and the rose in strenuous sport.
And, had it power, this verse would crown your game.

'On Sestus' shore, Leander's late resort,
Hero hath left no lamp to guide her love':
Is it eternal darkness that I court?

You were a spirit. Still I think you of
Some pure, strange kingdom where the purest move.

The Touch in the Living of the Dead [17]

Yet all those other hours are so much here
With a particular and proper light
As if time folded them in shining cloth,
Packed from the moth in attics of the night.

Here I must climb again, again the stair,
A creaking, crazy winding cylinder,
Up to the loft, where all those loves are laid.
Here this love's laid: and I afraid of her

Because the light is fading on her hair
And on the waning of our urgency,
As if the sea should fail upon the coast,
Fail like a ghost, the cruel persistent sea

Folded of memories that are the wear
Of those hours in the attic of the mind:
I call it mind or night; it is the fall
Of day's bright wall, and warns us we are blind

And have no feeling sight to stroke the bare
Bland and resistant nothingness that is
The hollow house of shape, untenanted
After we shed our sensualities.

Mind or night climbs. Seeks penetration where
(Great source and absence of all images!)
Its own light fills the darkness that it is,
Its own solidities its emptiness.

For all these other hours are so much here
And here or nowhere are the fled loves found...
Either all power upon this platform lies
Or horror cries from the corrupting ground.

Even here quick love must climb again the stair,
This quick hour climbing. A shivering youth and old,
Let me not totter now and fall from fear,
Your fire here kill me, dear: not there that cold.

Love Poem

In a reposing hand
White like the perfect snows
My hand now lies, and one
Resourceful as the rose,

Unmitigated grace
On which to concentrate
My hunted, haunted gaze:
Still trapped by Time too late,

Since careless Beauty that
I saw and did not see
Winds up my loose-skeined days
Round neat Eternity:

Lost, unlost, light retold,
Unfold, refold surprise.
Snow, snow. Snow rose. And glow
Of smoky campfire eyes.

Long is your path and mine
Twines off and gently fades,
But unafraid. Dark wine
Shall warm me in the Shades.

A Little Lament for Auden

In the winter of sorrow
    I looked in my glass
       (And I measured my glass):
I saw the years vanish,
    I saw my youth pass.

In the spring of disorder
    I gazed in the lake
       (It was blood-crimson lake)
I saw the buds shatter,
    I saw my heart break.

In the summer of ardour
    I bent to the rose
       (And it stirred and it rose):
I prised its lips open
    To drain my repose.

In the autumn of crispness
　　　I saw my sheaves bound
　　　（And moved back with a bound):
The sun in its circus
　　　Completed its round.

A late bird is flying
　　　To finish it all
　　　(I did finish it all):
Now one last cadenza,
　　　The fortunate fall.

A Lover's Quarrel

Now I have smashed it finally, I think.
And such sad harshness in her stare.
Eyes seem wet stone. And yet I drink
Life from her love as from the air.
Caught as half-throttled at the very brink
Of no more breathing, of the air withdrawn,
No use, it seems, to cry or rant or fawn,
All gesture frozen into falsity
Of, in that gaze, the knowledge of false me,
Seen as not here, that never had been there.
Then her hand touches mine, and I exist.
It was hurt, healing love and not despair.
Salt was the reconciling taste we kissed.
And my tears salt on hyacinthine hair.

To Paddy: For her Sixtieth Birthday

(Rye, August 1978)

This sixtieth year was still the first
　　　We saw low leaden prickly leaves,
High spiky stars at Sissinghurst:
A savaged church, an endless peace,
　　　A staked brown shore at Winchilsea;
　　　At Romney, sheep and never a cow;
　　　'Dorset, the Muses' pride' at Knole,
　　　Marshland, around the toy-sized church
At Fairfield, nibbled sheer as fleece,
　　　Twelfth Night in Ellen Terry's garden;
　　　And Bodiam heaved intact against
　　　The French who would attack no more;
Cosi Fan Tutte at Glyndebourne,
Too wet for supper on the grass
By greening nymph or mossy urn.
　　　One praised your two white streaks of hair:
Your wry smile would not say Alas!

190

My ageing heart has ceased to harden:
There is a wilderness of soul
Becomes a pleasance when its fenced.
Life like a fan lay widely open
When first we met; slow-closing now
But neatly still, and still unbroken.
Nor memory nor the glass deceives
Nor was the trip futility:
Outside Hong Kong with silver lurch
Drunk moons swum drunk on swelling waters:
Young mother of my son and daughters,
What mocking lips, what eyes forlorn,
What jade or what brocade you wore!
Sad eyes, and undersea a knell
For sunken stars in tatters torn.
Bad luck to pass upon the stair!
Together, down or up, our told tale tell.

Memory

I sing of something gone:
A corner or an edge
Out of the slant of sight,
Flowers by a window ledge

Hazed in a whirring light
Before the bulb clicks on:
On this side or on that?
But no light can switch on,

The room is somewhere else,
The twilight former day,
What window gives on fells
All slippery cutting-gray?

Sheep scrabble? Field of hay
Rough-barbered like a mat
New-plaited from Japan?
Brown-faced, a white straw hat,

The passing handyman
An Ainu from the north.
What bamboo-slats on Lake
Chusenji? On the Forth

What porthole waters break?
Confused, an ageing man
Remembering no one dream
Knows that the flash and flake

Are gappier than they seem.
He forgets age and friends,
Gropes forward as he can.
The blank signs post no ends.

It seems to end in snows
That blur the corridors.
Like thighs or like a rose.
It seems to end at doors.

Older

Lately the years have all come round
And hardly can come back again:
Something I lost has still been found:
Some of my tasks been tightly done
And will be done until the end.

Each child does well. That colleague smiles.
These students show civility.
Past, for a weakling, many a mile
I should erect a lofty brow
However near the thunder rolls.

Alas, old men are wearisome
And long before the senile stage:
I listen to my smart talk come,
The sterile maxims of a huge
Variety of All the Same.

Ideas that can shape a life
Have bitter roots, Polonius!
They thrust with pain to love or strife.
But lurking in the grandest house
For me all arrases are safe.

Yet I can strip the mask at least,
For meagre matter use no art:
I'm growing old, an awkward beast:
I'm slow and cannot make them out.
I lust to linger to the last!

Yes, I would linger if I could
At least to seem serene and brave,
Freshets beneath my grittiest mood
(And not be left all dry of love
Before the last late light decayed.)

High Dam, Finsthwaite, Westmorland, in October [18]

The time comes when the leaf must fall,
No wind but from the sycamore.
I see and faintly hear five more.
A larch at hand stands like a tall
Girl green skirts wide as if to make
A curtsy: beech-leaves corn-flake
Crisp; the birch tree leaves are all
Like small gold coins; floating on the tarn
Sodden to brown towards the greedy fall.
Unfallen rowan berries seem
Ruffled in their mirror dream.
Across the water's breadth the sprawl
Of death's brown bracken. Unfurled
Oakroots twist, wide, grasping, snarled,
And far the canvas-tearing call
Of rooks, small chirrups near. Stones
Avoid black mud, risk broken bones:
Slippy downhill and uphill haul.
Sit by cracked pallid bark and gaup;
Thick moss below, pale lichen up.
Upthrusting rock a trap and wall.
Over a bridge, field path, bullocks.
Reach Finsthwaite's one long street: relax.
We cannot always catch the ball
But our opponent throws it high,
High up still still, piled clouded sky.
The day comes when the leaf must fall.

Translations

For reasons of space, only a brief selection from many translations can be
included here.

Two Epigrams and a Little Elegy

(from Martial)

1

I don't like you, Sabidius, and cannot make clear just why:
But this much I can make clear. I don't like you.

2

They say Cinna is writing little verses against me:
Someone whom nobody reads is not really writing.

3

Fronto dead father, dead mother Flacilla, this little
    Girl, my kisses and sweets, I hand over
To you lest little Erotion shake at black shadows
    Or huge jaws of the Tartarean hound.
She would now have completed six foggy winters
    Had she lived only six more days.
Among old watchers like you let her play and wanton
    And with bubbling lips still lisp my name.
Turf, press not soft bones stiffly; nor on her,
    Earth, lie heavy; she was not heavy on thee.

Horace Odes

Book One

IX

Look at the shine of snow up there upon
Soracte, where the labouring boughs
    Sag with their load, and bleak
    Winter has blocked the streams.

Here, melt this rigour, scattering logs
High on the hearth; then trundle out,
    Grandly, the Sabine jars
    Of strong wine, four years old.

Leave to the gods the rest; who, when
They have allayed upon the boiling deep
    These skirmishers, frail ash
    And cypress cease to shake.

Stop searching into sad to-morrow and
What day Luck now may grant, count that
    As cash, Child, do not scorn
    Gay dalliance or the dance

So long as sour old age his distance keeps.
Now in the Campus Martius and the squares
    Is the time for twilight
    Whispers of assignation

For the laugh from a far off corner
Of a lurking girl who defends her
    Forearm and her fingers
    In a mock-modest way.

Ovid: Amores, 1,5

Sultry it was, and the day had passed its noontide:
    I stretched myself on the middle of my bed.
One shutter of the window open, I had closed the other:
    What light came through was such as you find in woods
Or a glow like dusk's with the sun just disappearing,
    Or like night just gone, and daylight not yet here.
It was such a light as would suit a backward maiden
    Whose shy shame hopes to find some covering—
And, in fact, Corinna came, in a girdled tunic,
    And her fair hair flowing on each side of her neck,

The very spit of the way the great Semiramis
      Went to her bed, and much-embraced Lais.
I tore her gown off—not that it veiled her greatly;
      But she struggled a bit to be covered by it still,
But, even as she fought, not wholly hoping to conquer;
      I won the fight, since she did not wish to win.
She stood before me with her thin gown fallen:
      In all her body I could find no stain.
What shoulders I saw (and I touched them, too), what arms
      And her paps' roundness—how ripe they were to be pressed!
What a level plain, under her breast, her belly;
      What grand, great flanks; and what a youthful thigh!
Need I catalogue details? I saw nothing unlovely,
      And her naked body I crushed to my naked own.
Write the rest for yourselves!
              Tired, at last, we slept quietly.
      May such a noontide often come my way!

Catullus: V

Dear Lesbia, let us live and love,
Never thinking twopence of
All these grumbling grim old men,
Suns go down, come up again:
Down but once goes our brief light
Into one perpetual night.
A thousand kisses, then a hundred,
Then a thousand and a hundred,
A hundred on a thousand pour!
When we've many thousand more
Let us muddle up the score.
Bad men might count every kiss
And might envy us our bliss.

Catullus: XXII

Varus, you know Suffenus well. He is
Handsome, and quite a wit, and nicely mannered,
And the most copious scribbler in the world.
He must have written quite ten thousand verses,
Or more, and not like other folk on scraps,
But on imperial paper, in new rolls,
New bosses, fine red ribbon, parchment covers,
All ruled with lead, and all smoothed out with pumice.
And when you read these, this smooth pretty fellow
Suddenly seems a goatherd or a navvy:
It's so absurd and such a total change.

What shall we say about this? Here's a man
More than just bright and gay and affable
Who suddenly becomes a hick of hicks
Taking to poetry: yet a man who's never
Really so happy as when writing poems:
That's what he likes and worships in himself.
Well, we all fall this way. There's not a person
Whom in some matter you can fail to see
To be Suffenus. Each has his own pet maggot:
We cannot see what hangs behind our backs.

Versions from Catullus

XLIII

Lady, of not the littlest nose,
Nor prettiest foot, nor blackest eyes,
Nor longest fingers, nor of dryest
Mouth nor quite lady like discourse—
You Formian bankrupt's fine kept bit!
The Province boasts about you, does it,
And says my Lesbia's rather like you?
O polished, O perceptive age!

LVII

O Caelius Lesbia who was mine that Lesbia
That very Lesbia whom alone Catullus
Loved far more than himself and all his folk,
Now at the cross-roads now in dark black alleys
Gluts the last spawn of lordly minded Remus!

LXX

She says there's no one she would marry rather
Than me, no not if Jove himself should ask her.
She says so. What they say when we are eager
On wind we should inscribe, or rapid water.

XCII

Lesbia is always slandering me and never
Silent about me: I am sure she loves me.
How? By my own case. For I run her down
Continually, and I am sure I love her.

LXXIV

I hate and love. How can that be, you ask me.
I don't know, but I feel it, and it's torture.

Catullus: LXXVI

If there's some pleasure in remembering
the decent things one did (that one felt true,
and broke no serious oath, and in no compact
used the god's greatness for deceiving men),
then, in a long life, many joys, Catullus,
are surely due you for your squandered love!
All gentle things a man can say or do
in love, by you have all been said or done:
all, to a thankless heart entrusted, perished.

Why do you still extend your area of
self-torture? Why not stiffen up, draw back,
and cease—the gods dislike it—to be wretched?
It's hard to quench an old love suddenly:
it's hard, indeed, but what you've got to do:
you must do this, whether you can or not!
Gods, if there's pity in you, or if ever
to any deathbed you brought any comfort,
have pity on poor me! Was my life honest?
Then snatch away this plague and ruin from me—
alas, this slackness in my deepest joints,
creeping that drives my heart's delight away!
I ask no longer this: for my love, her love:
nor wish she'd wish, though vainly, to be chaste.
I want mere health: to lay down this vile sickness.
If I've observed decorum, gods, grant this!

Tibullus: Book 1, Elegy 1

Hoards let others heap of tawny gold
And grip of good ploughed land, their greedy acres,
Whom steady watch for near marauders scares
And war's dour pulsing drum repels from sleep!
My humble lot grant me a humdrum life
And grant my hearth a steady-shining fire!
For me, may I be happy to live on a little
And not forever be pledged to the long march
But avoid the dogday heats in a tree's shadow
Upon a bank with water running by;
Nor feel it shame to handle the hoe sometimes
Myself, nor to jab at the slow ox with a goad;
Nor a great hardship to lift a lamb or a kid
Left by its dam, and myself carry it homeward.

Let myself, at the due time, graft the young vines
Like a true hodge, and deftly dig in the fruit trees;
So let Hope not cheat me, but always give me corn
Heaped high, and must foamy in a full vat.

For I pray, at least: wherever the garlands are hung,
By the lonely stump in the field, or on the crossways stone;
And a due share of my fruit that each year ripens
Is always set aside for the god of the farms.
Blond Ceres, do you, too, take from my lands a spiky
Wreath to be hung up by your temple doors;
And let ruddy Priapus be put as a guard in the fruit trees
To scare away the birds with his nasty hook!
Ye, too, of a rich soil once, now of a poor,
The guardians, receive your gifts, my Lares!
Once a slain heifer was pledge for unnumbered cattle;
Now a poor lamb is hostage for my narrow fields.
A lamb shall fall, the country loons around
Shall cry: 'Hail, harvests, Lares, and good wine!'
But ye, thievish wolves, my scanty flocks,
I pray, respect (great herds give proper prey!)
Here for my herdsman I make the year's lustration.
Appease with sprinkled milk the holy Bounds!
Be with me, Gods! Nor from a humble board
And clean earth platters, scorn these, my gifts!
(Earthen at first the earliest farmers made
Their dishes, shaping them from easy clay.)

It's not as if I asked for my fathers' portion
That high-heaped harvests brought them long ago!
A small field's yield is enough; it's enough to lie
On my own divan, to stretch on the usual bed.
How I delight, as I lie, in the wind's rage
And at having my dear one safe in my gentle arms;
Or when Auster lets out of the bag his icy torrents
To sleep secure to the tune of the falling rain!
This lot be mine; his, rightly, wealth, who can
Bear the sea's fury and the dreary rains!
Oh, let what gold and what emerald there is go perish
Rather than one girl weep for my going away!
It suits you, Messalla, to battle on sea and on land
So that your gates may be showy with enemy trophies.
A trophy myself, I am bound in the chains of a beauty —
I sit like a doorman in front of her obstinate doors!
Praise isn't *my* passion. Delia, only with you
Let me stay, may the world call me weakling and slack.

And on you let me look, my last hour striking,
And clasp you, dying, with a failing hand.
You will weep for me then
(On my bed that will have to be burned).

You will give me your kisses mixed with your sad tears.
You will weep; your bosom is not encased in iron
Nor with your tender heart does one find flint.
And from my burying, no brave boy at all
Nor pure young girl shall bear dry orbs away.
Yet, Delia, spare—oh, fear to vex my spirit—
Your soft young cheeks then and your loose, wild hair.

Meanwhile, the Fates permit it, join we loves!
Too soon comes Death, his head all cowled in dark:
Too soon slack Age, when it will not be decent
To love, or speak soft things with greying hairs!
Now, now, pursue light love, while it's still no shame
To break down doors, and hearty brawls delight us!
In love, I'm both captain and private: trumpet and flags.
Away, bear your gashes to greedier men,
And your gains, too! I, safe on my garnered heap,
Your wealth despise, as I despise your hunger.

Homage to Aulus Albius Tibullus: Book 1, Elegy 5

How well I'd bear the break, my anger spoke it:
Nothing more distant than defiance now!
Now, with a quick and clever boy to whip me,
I'm whirling like a top across the flags!

Brand my wild heart, and hurt it, that hereafter
It love not bragging: tame my bristling words!
And yet be kind. How once we put together
Our heads, made furtive plots, were fond, recall!
Think, when you lay cast down by wretched sickness,
Who was it sprinkled cleansing sulphur round,
And who invoked, lest mournful dreams beset you,
Quiet sleep, thrice scattering the sacred meal?
Cowled, in loose tunic, through the small hours' silence,
Who at the crossroads made the ninefold vow?
This payment mine, another has the profit,
Lucky, who draws the interest on my prayers!
I feigned, poor frantic man (the gods unfriendly!)
I should be happy then, if you were safe.

Life on the land! Let Delia watch my harvests,
While on the hot, hard floor they thresh the corn,
Or watch the clusters in the full vat heaping
When rapid feet tread out the shiny must;
And learn to count my flocks; and, a loving
Mistress, to dandle talkative small slaves;
Learn to give grapes as offering for vintage,
Spiked ears in pledge for corn, brimmed bowls for flocks.
She'll manage every man and every matter
And leave no task for me in all my house.
Messalla visits us...the sweetest apples
Delia will pluck him from the choicest trees:
Such a great man, she'll be an anxious hostess,
Prepare and serve his meals, a waiting maid!

Such were my dreams that now the crosswinds carry
To scatter in Amenia's scented vales!

Often with drink I seek to rout these sorrows,
But sorrow turns wine itself to tears,
Often with girls; but on joy's very margin
Love, that recalls my love, abandons me.
The one who leaves me then will talk of witchcraft,
And say — oh, shame! — you know unholy charms!
And yet it is not words that could bewitch me,
But looks, soft arms, and girlish golden hair:
Such to Haemonian Peleus once was Thetis,
The sea-blue Nereid on her bridled fish!
These charms could charm me!

                    Some rich lover wants you,
And his accomplice is some crafty bawd!
May blood defile her food, her mouth be bloody
As it gluts brewage mingled with much gall!
May ghosts around her ply, their plight bemoaning,
Yes, and the ghoul-bird skirl upon her roof!
Let her pluck grass from graveyards, dogged by hunger,
Seek pickings from the morsels left by wolves,
Howl through the streets with nothing round her middle,
Run at the crossways from wild yelping dogs!
So be it! A god confirms. Powers guard lovers.
Venus, renounced for no just cause, will rage.
So, Delia, leave this witch's griping lessons
In time, in time...
                    In love must riches win?
For your poor man is your most trusty servant,
Your poor man soonest cleaves to your soft side,
Your poor man, in the crush, a sturdy comrade,
Pushes your hips and somehow makes a way,
Your poor man will draw off your muddy leggings
And loose the coverings from your snowy feet.

(I sing in vain! Fine words will not win open
That door, who knocks must have a plenteous hand!)

You, who carry the day, of my fate be wary!
Light Luck turns lightly on her turning wheel.
Not in vain now one waits at the threshold,
Patient, and looks about him, and withdraws,
And seems to pass the house, but soon returning
Will hawk himself at Delia's very doors!
Sly Love has a dodge afoot. Be gay, I beg you,
While you can: your sloop still bobs in a clear sea!

Notes

1. 'Utopia and Ideology'

   'Utopia and Ideology' was published in *Home Town Elegy* in 1944; a later version with slight variations exists under the title 'Troy without Helen'.

2. 'Epistle to an Unhappy Friend'

   An earlier version of this poem exists, entitled 'Epistle to Anne Sprague' and beginning 'Anne dear, at my window now'. Anne Sprague was a young poet of promise whom G.S.F. helped during a time of personal difficulties.

3. 'Epistle to J.G.'

   François Maynard (1583-1646), follower of Malherbe.

4. 'Monologue for a Cairo Evening'

   'Larry' — Lawrence Durrell, who was working in Cairo at the time.
   'gully-gully trick' — 'gully-gully men' used to earn money on ships calling in at Port Said, bound for Suez, by doing disappearing tricks with birds.
   'John' — John Waller, the poet, who as Captain John Waller was G.S.F.'s superior officer at the Ministry of Information in Cairo.
   'Kay' — Kay Garland, a secretary at the Ministry of Information in Cairo, later killed when the bomb fell on the Guards Chapel in London.
   'Keith Douglas' — famous war-poet who fought in the Western Desert and was killed in the Normandy landings.
   'Erik' — Erik de Mauny, who was with the New Zealand Army in the Desert, now a well-known B.B.C. correspondent.
   'Alan' — Alan Arnold, at the time Chief Press Officer at the French Embassy in Cairo.
   'Cyril' — Cyril des Baux, pen name of Mohammed Sadiq Bey, an Egyptian essayist and playwright.
   'Tatiana' — Tatiana Hankiewicz, editor and secretary at the Ministry of Information in Cairo.

5. 'Metaphysical Epistle' and 'An Evening Half of Fog'

   These are both fragments dating from the 1940s and were sent to Ian Fletcher at Reading University.

6. 'Prayer for the New Year'

   This poem was written in the early 1950s. 'The war and rage of our world' may well refer to the Korean War which broke out while G.S.F. was in Japan.

7. 'Little Lament'

   'Mrs Nicoline Goodman, for whom this elegy was written, died in Tokyo in 1951. She came from a noble Polish family settled on the borders of the Ukraine. During the Second World War she was for a time a prisoner of the Russians but eventually was able to join the Polish forces in the Near East. Hence the allusions to castles on the plain as centres of defence against Tartar or Cossack invasions, and to her courage. She was a poet, in English, of very considerable promise. She was a very beautiful woman, and as a person combined in what I suppose is a typically Polish way, a childlike social gaiety with an unconscious aristocratic *hauteur* and, with a stoically fatalistic attitude towards life and history, a deep inner sadness.' — G.S.F.

8. 'Poetic Generations'

   The 'prophets' in the first stanza probably refers to the poets of the Left — Auden, Spender and Day Lewis — and their warnings against the rise of Fascism. The 'bards' may have been poets like Dylan Thomas and David Gascoygne who regarded the subconscious as a deep source of poetry. 'The new brisk young' is a reference to the 'Movement' poets of the 1950s: Philip Larkin, Kingsley Amis, Donald Davie and others.

9. 'The Poet on his Birthday'
   This is a revised version of 'For T.S. Eliot's Sixtieth Birthday', written in 1948.

10. 'Barrington in 1798'
    'Much, but not all of this, is almost a straight versification of some exciting paragraphs in Sir Jonah Barrington's *Memoirs,* a book which is as racy as Smollett, but also an indispensable source for understanding Yeats's "hard-riding country gentlemen". He liked tall stories and this one is artistically convincing whether or not historically true.'—G.S.F.

11. 'Instead of an Elegy'
    This was written in the emotional days following the assassination of John Kennedy when G.S.F. was teaching in the U.S.A. The images in the poem derive from watching the televising of the funeral.

12. 'How the Heart Grows Cold'
    A later version probably written in the 1960s of a long poem with seven sections first written in the 1940s. The poem printed here originally formed sections 3 and 5.

13. 'A Lesson in Humanity for the Children, out of Aristotle's *Poetics*'
    This was written for the Leicester Race Relations Board Newsletter in 1970, at a time when race relations were uneasy in the Midlands.

14. 'University Road Graveyard'
    Leicester University is built on a smallish site and lacks land for expansion. This poem was inspired by a rumour that, after the lapse of the statutory length of time, the University would build on the graveyard opposite, on the other side of University Road—probably quite unfounded. It is possible that the form was suggested by T.W. Rolleston's poem 'Clonmacnoise', in *The Oxford Book of English Verse,* edited by Yeats.

15. 'Colleagues and Students'
    'The allusion in the fourth stanza to a "hound-in-cry's voice" is to Yeats's poem to the Duchess of Wellington, "Hound Voice" —a poem which, if it is to come across, needs expression rather than exposition. The broader theme is the very mixed feelings which teachers have about their students, their colleagues, and above all, themselves.'—G.S.F.

16. 'A Napkin with Veronica's Face, Not Christ's'
    'Veronica Forrest-Thompson died in April 1975, at the beginning of her twenty-eighth year. She was then a lecturer at Birmingham University. She left a book called *Poetic Artifice,* and this piece is an attempt at the kind of artefact she might have liked, with allusions to her favourite poems, and poets. The form is the mock-sonnet in *terza-rima* of Shelley's *West Wind.*'—G.S.F.

17. 'The Touch in the Living of the Dead'
    This poem in a slightly different version was first published under the title 'Metaphysical Elegy' in 1948. A revised version written in the mid-1970s, with the title 'Lost Loves', carried the following footnote by G.S.F.: 'Written in not such a tidy version, many years ago but I never chose to publish it. I think it sounds all right but ought for the sound to have a deeper sense than it seems to—something about all actual love being haunted by the memory of past love and, a favourite theme of Yeats's, an intensive passion going with a growing physical inadequacy. But perhaps there is also something slightly crazy about the past being physically explorable and about the living acting as real mediators between us and, embodiers of the loved dead.'
    This final version, 'The Touch in the Living of the Dead', was published in Leicester University's *Poetry Worksheet* No. 4 in 1977.

18. 'High Dam, Finsthwaite, Westmorland, in October'
    This poem, an exact account of a walk near Finsthwaite, when his strength was failing, was unfinished at G.S.F.'s death. This version was put together from drafts lying on his desk.

Index of First Lines